Lessons in IT Transformation

Lessons in IT Transformation

Technology Expert to Business Leader

LARRY BONFANTE

WILEY

John Wiley & Sons, Inc.

Published by John Wiley & Sons, Inc., Hoboken, New Jersey.
Published simultaneously in Canada.

For general information on our other products and services or for technical support, please contact our Customer Care Department within the United States at (800) 762-2974, outside the United States at (317) 572-3993 or fax (317) 572-4002.

Wiley also publishes its books in a variety of electronic formats. Some content that appears in print may not be available in electronic books. For more information about Wiley products, visit our website at www.wiley.com.

Library of Congress Cataloging-in-Publication Data:
Bonfante, Larry
 Lessons in IT transformation : technology expert to business leader / Larry Bonfante.
   p. cm.
 Includes index.
 ISBN 978-1-118-00447-0 (cloth); 978-1-118-04447-6 (ebk); 978-1-118-04448-3 (ebk); 978-1-118-04450-6 (ebk)
 1. Information technology—Management. 2. Leadership. I. Title.
 HD30.2.B657 2011
 004.068'4—dc22   2010053513

Printed in the United States of America

10 9 8 7 6 5 4 3 2 1

To the greatest teachers in my life:

My mother, Josephine, who taught me
the meaning of selflessness

My grandfather, Jerome, who taught me
the meaning of integrity

My wife, Denise, who taught me the
meaning of strength

My daughters, Danielle and Christine,
who taught me what really matters in life

Thank you for your lessons and your love.

Contents

Preface

Every generation must deal with the challenges of a constantly changing world. Although many of the issues and dynamics we face may change over time, the one variable that remains constant is the need for quality leaders to help us navigate difficult and uncharted waters. There have been countless books written on the subject of leadership. I have read many of these books and learned a great deal from the experience. While all of them were valuable, no book written by another human being can capture an individual's personal evolution as a leader. This book is meant to share my own journey to date in the hope that the lessons I have learned will be of value to other leaders. It is also written from the point of view of a CIO so that it can be of specific value to technology leaders. It is by no means meant to be the definitive tome on the topic of leadership. Many of the lessons contained within these pages are certainly reflected in other books on this topic.

What Is a CIO?

CIO is a term that means many things in various organizations. The idea of creating a position of chief information officer is about 25 years old. CIOs have historically been entrusted with operating the technology services and assets of modern organizations. However, today more than ever, the shift in focus is away from simply being a "utility provider" who keeps the lights on. The modern CIO has to be an evangelist, an innovator, a revenue producer, a consumer expert, and an executive relationship manager. These are skills that are not always naturally inborn into many IT executives who have grown up through the ranks of technology organizations. We will focus on the traits and talents that you must be able to incorporate into your portfolio if you hope to be a successful CIO in the year 2011 and beyond.

It's Common Sense

Over the years, I have noticed that the teams who win on Sunday are not the teams with the best trick plays, but rather those who block and tackle the best. Much of what is contained in this book will seem like common sense, but as a wise man once told me, common sense is not that common! It is amazing how often we don't leverage the lessons we've learned over time to improve our relationships and outcomes. This book is not intended to impress the reader with complex concepts. It is meant to help share the simple concepts that I have seen make a meaningful difference in leading successful teams.

The older I get, the more I realize that I will always be a student of leadership. I am not arrogant enough to believe that I am an expert or that I have all the answers. My desire is to continue to learn until my last day on this planet. I hope that readers will take away from my experiences some useful bits of knowledge that will help them become a better leader and help them to develop the leadership qualities in the people around them. As a person who has a great passion about the subject of leadership, writing this book has been a labor of love.

Introduction

Why should I read this book? Be honest—that's what you are really trying to figure out before you decide to invest the time and money required to read any book. There are thousands of books available on the topic of leadership. Why is this book different, and why should you care? Here are a few answers to your question.

First of all, this book is written for the IT professional as its stated audience. It focuses on the topic of leadership through the unique perspective of an IT practitioner. It is also written through the lens of an actively practicing CIO who lives the challenges of leading and managing a complex technology organization every day.

The book is also very different from many resources written for the IT community in that it focuses on what I lovingly refer to as the *human side* of IT leadership. Many IT executives have risen through the technical ranks and already have a great handle on leading IT projects, implementing technical solutions, and handling the day-to-day operations of a technology organization. What most CIOs or aspiring CIOs don't always have is a great deal of experience or focused education in dealing with the human elements of leading an organization that ultimately will decide whether you, as well as your organization, succeed. In this book we will focus on real, pragmatic issues that are critical for executive success. These topics include:

- Helping to create a vision that your team will embrace
- The real purpose of IT—driving business value

- Developing effective communication skills
- Becoming an effective relationship manager
- Developing the people on your team for maximum contribution
- Leading a major change effort
- Creating an atmosphere of partnership with your people, clients, and vendors
- Developing the qualities of great leaders
- Sustaining success once it's achieved

These topics are critical to executive success but are not often taught in MBA programs or easily learned on the job. I will cram nearly 30 years of lessons from the school of hard knocks into these pages in the hope that you can avoid having to invest as much time (and make as many mistakes!) as I have.

Finally, the book has two major focuses—helping the individual evolve from a technical expert to a business executive and helping his/her organization evolve from a utility service provider to a trusted business partner that drives true business value. If these are goals you hope to accomplish, then this is the right book for you at the right time.

First Things First: What Is Leadership?

Before we get into the "nuts and bolts" of what is involved in transforming an IT organization, we will spend some time defining some key concepts. Specifically, we will focus on the following concepts:

- ☐ Defining what I mean by leadership
- ☐ Comparing and contrasting leadership and management
- ☐ Reviewing common misperceptions regarding leadership
- ☐ Examining the critical roles that a transformational leader has to play

Defining Leadership

There are probably as many definitions of leadership as there are people who have an interest in the topic. Many of us have formed our thoughts and definitions based on the people in our lives from whom we have learned our lessons of leadership. For many people, the image of leadership comes along with formal power and authority. For others, it elicits a vision of eloquent orators who can inspire with their thoughts and words. Some may conjure up emotional pictures of military leaders or sports coaches who "fire up" the troops.

What we will explore in this book is the fact that there is no one approach or definition to leadership. Individuals bring their own unique personality and talents to their position of leadership. In trying to define leadership, perhaps a good place to start is to differentiate between two very important but different things—leadership and management.

Leadership versus Management

Before we begin our discussion on leadership, it is important to differentiate between the concepts of leadership and management. Many people will share that they think good leadership is more important to an organization's success than excellent management. This is akin to saying that speed is more important to an athlete than strength. The truth of the matter is that both are critical to success.

Over the almost 30 years I have worked in the industry, I have come to realize how rare excellent management is and how rarely it is appreciated and rewarded. In many organizations, when an individual contributor excels, he or she is promoted to a management position. The thought process is that if someone is proficient in a functional area, that person would naturally be able to manage others who are focused in that area of endeavor. Nothing could be further from the truth. Although some people clearly can make this leap, excellence in any endeavor and the ability to manage people in the same discipline are two very different sets of muscles. Working in the field of IT, it is sometimes painful to watch very talented technical people who entered the field because of certain skills and personality traits being asked to act in what can only be described as unnatural ways to try to manage the efforts of other technical contributors.

In my experience, there is a dearth of quality managers. People who can help teams execute and deliver results are a precious commodity. Many organizations do not value or reward excellent managers. However, without these people, companies would never accomplish the results required to achieve success. Therefore, in our discussion of leadership versus management, I want to be clear that I value both capabilities. It's just that they are very different things.

Picture This

How many times have you seen this movie play out? An extremely talented technologist does a stellar job on a critical project. As a "reward" for his efforts, he gets promoted into a management role. Suddenly, this incredibly intelligent and talented person finds himself in a whole new world. Instead of being able to leverage his technical acumen and quantitative skills to get a job done, he is asked to manage people who just a week ago were his peers. Some of these people resent his promotion and his new role. He doesn't know how to relate to people who were colleagues but now are in his employ. No one has trained him on how to adapt to this new role.

Even worse, his introversion and quiet demeanor, which were assets up until now, are viewed as challenges as he struggles to communicate his vision for the team and how he hopes to execute against it. Being quiet and reserved is mistaken for lacking leadership qualities required to manage the team. He hasn't developed the relationships required to build credibility and confidence in the people above him in the organization. Months go by, and instead of delegating critical tasks, he tries to do it all himself. His people are disgruntled. His management is disappointed. He is frustrated. Finally, a year into his tenure, he is called into his manager's office and relieved of his responsibilities.

(continued)

(Continued)

Part of him is shocked—how could I have gone from being a star to being a bum in a year? Part of him is actually relieved to not have to fit into a role for which he was clearly not suited. He has to take his severance check and explain to his family that he is unemployed and has to look for a new job. Sound familiar? Could it happen to you?

To me, the simplest way to differentiate between leadership and management is to identify three questions that must be answered for teams to succeed. The first two questions are issues of leadership. The third is a question of management.

Question #1: Where Are We Going?

The first question that must be answered by a leader is, "Where are we going?" The essence of leadership is setting the direction for the organization. Leaders must work with their people to explain their destination. There is an old expression that if you don't know where you are going, you might not like where you wind up! The first responsibility of a leader is to know where you are going so you can communicate this direction with your team. Many books I have read on the topic of leadership stop there! They feel that the primary responsibility of a leader is to determine and communicate the team's destination. I think that there is a second related question that leaders are required to answer.

Through the Lens of the CIO—The Need for CIOs to Inspire

I can remember the first time I heard the idea of the CIO having to inspire the organization. It was at an industry conference, and we had a keynote speaker who suggested that leaders must inspire their people to greatness. Why is this a daunting challenge for most CIOs?

Let's think about where most CIOs come from. Many of us grew up through the ranks of the technology organization. Our skill sets were in areas such as business analysis, systems development, and process management. In school, we were more likely to be attracted to topics such as math and science than to subjects such as psychology and philosophy, which many of us probably viewed as "fluff" courses. (I will make the admission that I was a dual major when I got my undergraduate degree, pursuing both economics and psychology!) We are most comfortable with quantitative, hard-core, tangible items that we can see and touch. We are often binary in our thinking—after all, computer science is at its core based on ones and zeros! We count lines of code; we install and program switches and routers—no bull happening here!

All of a sudden, many of us are placed in positions where we have to lead and "inspire" people. Inspiration is the stuff of evangelists and football coaches, not managers of technology. But like it or not, people only perform at their greatest potential when they are inspired.

One of the big mistakes many CIOs make when attempting to inspire is to think that they have to come up with some magic words that awaken the greatness that resides in all of us. We have to know exactly what to say to light the fire in people. Truth be told, individuals have their own motivators that inspire them. All we have to do is figure out what those things are for the people we lead and find a way to align our vision and our mission to the things that drive people. You can call that inspiration. Motivation is really an "inside job." Our role is not to create the things that inspire people but simply to make people understand how what we are doing connects with what *already* inspires them.

Another challenge many CIOs have is trying to develop the *cult of personality*. Some of us (like me) happen to become

(*continued*)

(Continued)

extroverts over time. I started out an introvert, but based on life experiences and situations have become far more extroverted and comfortable in dealing with people than many CIOs are naturally wired to be. But what about those of us (and this is probably the great majority) who are introverted? After all, there is a reason we went into IT as opposed to sales or marketing. What do we do about the introverts? Remember that inspiration is about your people, not about you! What CIOs have to do is to be real, to be human, and to be themselves. People can smell a phony from a mile away. Therefore, trying to be a cheerleader if this is not your nature will most certainly backfire. Be yourself. Be genuine. Speak from your heart in a way that people know is true to who you are, and they will respect you for it. Don't try to be someone you're not. Be yourself—but be your *best* self and work to bring out the best in each of the people you lead. This is the true essence of inspiring people, not being some loud, fiery B.S. artist!

Question #2: Why Are We Going There?

Getting others to support a shared vision requires that they buy into what you are trying to accomplish. A big part of ensuring that this happens is answering for them why you plan to go in a stated direction. When I was starting out, the roles of management and labor were very clear. As a member of the staff, you were simply expected to do as you were told by your management. No questions asked! However, things have changed. Most of us lead "volunteer" armies! People can pick and choose among many opportunities and employers. If you truly expect to get people to rally around you and accomplish great things, you need to help them envision why you want to go toward your planned destination.

In setting the course and explaining why you are headed for your destination, every leader must be prepared to answer two parts of this question:

1. *Why are you as the leader planning to go in this direction?* Of all the places you could go, why is this the best place? What about this destination makes it special, different, important? What about this destination inspires you and energizes you to put forth the effort required to arrive there?
2. *Why should the people on your team want to go there with you?* This question might be even more important for the people you lead. What about this trip speaks to their needs, hopes, dreams, and desires?

We will explore both parts of the "why" question in this book. The bottom line is that most people want you to explain to them, "What's in it for me?" Unless you can create the same level of motivation and excitement in them that you must personally exhibit, at best you will get lukewarm buy-in and less than full effort. Great objectives require great effort and great passion. Getting people excited about the possibilities for them as individuals as well as for the team is critical to getting the required level of involvement.

Question #3: How Do We Get There?

Once a leader has articulated a vision of where the team is going and why the members of that team should be excited about going there, management must ensure that the team executes. It's the manager's job to help lay out the plan for how to get from where we are to where we hope to arrive. Management is accountable for working with the team to chart the actual course for the intended destination—identifying and planning the required steps needed to get from where we are to where we hope to go. Managers need to work with their team to provide them the guidance, support, tools, feedback, motivation, and re-wards to ensure that the team can bridge the gap from the cur-rent state to the intended future destination.

Misconceptions about Leadership

Over the years I have met a number of people who aspired to positions of leadership for all the wrong reasons. First of all, leadership is not really about position. It is all about influence. In many organizations the people who truly lead by influence do not necessarily show up at the top of the organization chart. We will talk more about this is a little while.

Following is a list of the common misconceptions:

- *Leadership is all about the rewards.* Many people aspire to a position of leadership because of "what's in it for them." They see leadership as a destination to arrive at where they will receive the perks they feel they deserve. This includes financial rewards, recognition, having people do things for them, and more. They view leadership as a position of privi-lege. These "wanna-be" leaders do not recognize that lead-ership is a responsibility, not a privilege.
- *Leaders are served.* If you ever watch great leaders, you will see that first and foremost, they thrive on serving others. Their purpose is to help the team succeed. Their focus is on working to ensure the personal development and success of the members of their teams. Early in my career, I heard an expression that has stuck with me throughout the years: "When you are a leader, it's never about you!" A true leader is focused on the success, development, happiness of his or her people, clients and management. They are motivated by making a difference in the lives of others, not by accumulat-ing the accoutrements of power. Real leaders know that to lead is to serve, not to be served.

- *Leaders focus on achieving personal goals.* If you look at great leaders throughout history, you will notice a focus on helping others reach their potential—many times at the expense of making their own lives safer or more comfortable. Their entire thought process is about how they can help others achieve their goals. Great leaders know that there are no winners on a losing team. They know that the only success that matters is the team's success. That's why in most sports you rarely see a Most Valuable Player award given to a player whose team did not make the playoffs. If success is a team game, the focus cannot be on individual accomplishments.
- *Leadership means I've made it.* Ascending to a leadership position is not the last step of the journey but, rather, the first step to a new journey. Being promoted to a leadership role isn't an invitation to relax and enjoy the fruits of your labor. It is an invitation to roll up your sleeves and work to help your team chart a course for success. Leadership requires hard work and dedication but many new leaders think that they have arrived and can rest on their laurels.
- *Good managers are natural leaders.* As we've seen, leadership and management are two different sets of muscles. Being able to set a course and inspire people is a different set of skills than being able to work with people to plow the road that gets us to our desired destination. Both effective management and inspired leadership are required for success, but thinking one person automatically has both sets of skills is often a mistake.

Through the Lens of the CIO—The Peter Principle at Play

How many times have you seen someone who is incredibly talented at a position rewarded for their excellence by being promoted to a role for which they are neither prepared nor

(continued)

(Continued)

equipped? This is often referred to as the Peter Principle—in an organization, people get promoted up to their level of incompetence. Unfortunately, there is a particularly common and insidious version of this that happens to IT professionals.

Many IT professionals went into the field because of their personality types (often introverts) and the way they are naturally wired (logical, organized, curious, scientific thinkers). Their comfort with ideas, concepts, logic, and numbers far exceeds their comfort level with other human beings!

I had a person who I worked with, let's call him John. John was a brilliant technologist who was as dedicated and devoted as any person I've ever worked with. He was a tremendous individual contributor who was usually found smack dab in the middle of many of the successful projects we ran as an IT organization. John's "reward" for this excellence was to be promoted into a management position. What the brilliant leaders and human resource managers involved in this decision failed to take into account is the fact that leading and managing people require very different sets of muscles than being a technical contributor. No great thought was given as to whether John possessed the skills required to succeed in this new role. Furthermore, no great thought was given as to providing John the developmental opportunities, mentoring or support system to help him transition into the role of people leader. Many of the people John was asked to manage were peers of his in the organization. Some of them were older and more experienced than John and were resentful that this "whiz kid" was ascending up the corporate food chain faster than they had. John had always been a "straight shooter" who spoke his truth. He didn't have experience with the tact necessary to persuade people to see or do things a different way than they may have been comfortable doing them in the past. John started his new role with a great many strikes against him. He was thrown into a new world without a map of the terrain, a knowledge of the new language, or a plan as to how to do what seemed to him like a foreign set of responsibilities.

As we fast-forward the clock a year later, John's management was very disappointed. There were all kinds of comments made regarding his performance. "John had shown so much potential, I'm really surprised how badly he is struggling." "John has been a real disappointment; I expected much more from him." About 18 months after John had been promoted for being an exceptional contributor, he was let go from the organization. Very sad . . . let's move on!

Although John certainly contributed to some of the challenges he experienced, in many ways he was also a victim of the situation. He had been promoted into a role without any thought as to whether he had the temperament or abilities to play it effectively. There was no training, support, or mentoring provided to John, and his management, truth be told, were not effective leaders or managers of people themselves! There was plenty of blame to go around, but unfortunately the only person who suffered any fallout from this haste and poor decision was John! Have you seen this movie before? How many times?

In summary, leaders help their people understand where they are going and why they are going there and then empower them through effective management to figure out how to get there.

Leadership Roles

Every leader has to wear several hats. In order to effectively lead the process of change, a person must effectively play numerous roles at various junctures in the transformation process.

Business Executive

First and foremost, a CIO is a business executive. Anyone who has a "C" in the title is expected to function at an executive level and have the broad perspective of the entire organization when making decisions. Functional knowledge and experience is table stakes, not differentiators. Of course the chief marketing officer is an expert at marketing the products and services of the organization and understands how the company fits into the competitive landscape within which it plays. The CFO is expected to be able to master cash flow and determine how best to invest the organization's financial assets for both short-term liquidity and long-term growth. The CIO is expected to be able to leverage technical solutions and information assets to help drive the agenda for the organization. The real value added is when these business leaders can roll up their sleeves and pool both their collective business acumen as well as their specialized functional expertise to help strategize and drive value for the organization. First and foremost, if you want a seat at the table (an expression I can't stand), you have to know what to do once you get there!

Evangelist

A couple of years ago, I heard a presentation at a major technology conference at which I was speaking. The presenter stated that as a leader, it is imperative that you inspire the people on your team. *Inspiration* is not a word that most IT executives use that often. When we think of inspiration, we tend to flash back to fiery football coaches such as Knute Rockne, who exhorted his team to win one for the Gipper. Or perhaps you reflect back on the great charismatic orators of our time, such as Dr. Martin Luther King Jr., John F. Kennedy,, or President Barack Obama—people who can move others with their vision and their passion.

When I heard this presentation, I must admit that I was a bit intimidated at first. I consider myself many things, but *inspirational* is not necessarily one of the adjectives I would use to describe myself.

However, if you look up the word *inspiration* in Webster's Dictionary you will find several definitions. Here is one of them:

The action or power of moving the intellect or emotions.

Let's reflect on this definition and relate how it applies to effective leaders.

Leadership indeed requires moving the intellect or emotion. Leaders must convince, persuade, and influence people to devote their energies and talents to the pursuit of a worthy objective. Leaders must also reach into a person's emotional place to hit a chord that motivates them to give their best. Leaders are always working to influence the people around them and suggest approaches and ideas that they need others to embrace and pursue. When inspiration is put in these terms, it becomes a little less intimidating and a lot more practical to consider.

Therefore, I would submit to you that the first role that a leader must play is the role of evangelist. Leaders must inspire the key stakeholders within their sphere of influence to embrace new ideas, new approaches, new destinations and directions, and must somehow get the best of people's minds and souls to drum up the required enthusiasm, energy, and commitment needed to drive transformational change.

Captain of the Ship

The next role a leader must play is what I will refer to as being the captain of the ship. In Chapter 2 we will focus a great deal on the concept of creating and embracing a vision. Effective leaders, in essence, set the course for the vessels they are piloting.

They must get people to buy into traveling toward the stated port of destination at the exclusion of other potential destinations that might look more attractive at face value or seem easier to reach. Leaders must also keep people focused on the destination when the winds blow against them and the waters get choppy. They must ensure that the crew is prepared for the long journey of transformation and that there is enough esprit de corps to guard against any potential mutiny in the face of difficulty.

Teacher and Coach

I have seen countless CIOs frustrated by the fact that members of their boards of directors or their executive management teams *don't get it.* They bristle at how little their constituents seem to understand about technology and how it is implemented, and they somehow feel superior because they have a lexicon that others seem to not understand. They also get frustrated when their people make mistakes or fall into traps that may seem obvious to a more experienced person.

One of the critical roles of any effective leader is to be a patient and willing teacher. Consider these four factors:

1. You must be willing and able to explain complex technical ideas and solutions in laymen's terms.
2. You must be willing to educate key stakeholders not only on what you are trying to accomplish but also on why it matters to them and why your approach would be the best.
3. You need to make very accomplished and successful people feel more comfortable living in a world that seems foreign to them and where they may feel inadequate or even stupid.
4. You need to help mentor your people and allow them to grow and develop the skills they need to evolve into effective leaders in their own right.

When a person first learns to drive a car, there seems to be dozens of things that must be done at the same time—check your mirrors, step on the gas, hit your turn signal, check your speed, the list goes on and on. An experienced driver does all of these things without thinking about them. As a matter of fact, most of us drive to work and can't recall much about how we got from point A to point B, as if we were in a trance! But if you ever watch a parent trying to teach a teenager how to drive, you will quickly realize that the things we take for granted and can do in our sleep are things that need to be taught and explained. If you are a sports fan, you may have come to the realization that some of the greatest players often fail when they attempt to transition into the role of coach. For an extremely gifted athlete, it must be very difficult to understand why the young players he is trying to coach can't do the things he was able to accomplish with such ease. Often, the best coaches are those who were, at best, average players. They know what it's like to have to learn and struggle to develop a skill. They have more patience and a greater level of empathy and willingness to teach and explain basic principles to their players.

Part of being an effective coach is also knowing when to teach, when to correct, and when to allow people to fall down and brush themselves off. One of the hardest things to do as a coach or parent is to watch someone you care about make a mistake and stand by as they skin their knees. There is an overwhelming desire to say, "Don't do that! I tried it and it didn't work for me. It's a mistake, and it will cost you." However, part of teaching people is allowing them to discover their own truths and learn their own lessons. Feeling the emotions of short-term failure can be a powerful learning tool. There is a story of a young boy who was watching a caterpillar struggle to break out of its cocoon to become a butterfly. He watched as the tiny creature fought hard to break free from the chrysalis. Eventually, he couldn't take it anymore and made a cut in the cocoon for the creature to break through. When it emerged, instead of flying away, the butterfly dropped to the ground. It was unable to fly because it lacked the strength in its wings that would have been developed as it worked to break through of its own volition. Part of being a coach and teacher is knowing when to allow your people to make mistakes, struggle, and strengthen their wings so that they have the wherewithal to be able to fly on their own.

Cheerleader

An often-overlooked role of great leaders is that of cheerleader. Most of us have grown up in a hard world where we are expected to be strong, tough, self-motivated adults. Perhaps we didn't receive a lot of accolades or attaboys from people in authority positions. People are often raised in a way that values independence and individuality. That is all well and good. However, many of us can remember a childhood experience where a coach or teacher said a kind word or recognized an accomplishment. How did that make us feel? Can you remember being really down and feeling you would never be able to accomplish an important goal when perhaps a friend or parent told you to hang in there a little longer and eventually the tide would turn in your favor? Being a cheerleader for your team simply means that you recognize their efforts, give them a pat on the back, and take the time and effort to catch them doing something right and recognize them for it. We all want to feel appreciated and valued. An occasional pat on the back or supportive word at a difficult time might mean more to a person than you can ever know.

Strategist

Part of being an effective business leader involves helping to develop and lay out the strategic direction for your organization. This includes not only understanding your company's stated mission and direction, as well as its strengths and weaknesses, but also understanding the competitive landscape within which you play to see how to best position your organization for success. Today more than at any time in the past, technology and information are absolutely critical components to the strategy of any organization in any industry. Whether it is leveraging consumer knowledge to more effectively position your products or services or using social media to market and publicize your efforts, technology is at the center of how we live and do business. Therefore, the CIO not only needs a *seat at the table* but also the will to drive the strategy for competing in the twenty-first-century marketplace. IT is no longer a backroom function and a cost of doing business; if leveraged effectively, it can be a competitive differentiator that spells the difference between market leadership and bankruptcy!

Innovator

Now more than ever, the IT function is expected to help drive a company's innovation engine. Whether that means leveraging technology to market and communicate key messages, using business intelligence to help drive strategic usage of assets, or ensuring that your executive team is able to collaborate anywhere at any time, innovation is an expectation. It's not enough for IT to enable innovation. Part of our leadership role is to drive innovation and recommend creative uses of technology to help a company differentiate itself in a crowded and competitive marketplace.

Shop Foreman

Many IT executives bristle at the thought of IT as a utility. I agree that if all IT is to an organization is a utility, that organization has done a poor job of leveraging what can be a key value creator.

However, let's remember that in any hierarchy of value, the only way the top rung is reached is by solidifying the bottom steps on the ladder. Ignore the utility aspect of IT at your own peril! Let's see how many strategic conversations your executive team is having with you if e-mail is constantly down. No one will take you seriously as the architect of business strategy if you can't even keep the lights on in your own house. I am not suggesting that your focus should be on the tactical aspects of commodity services. I am simply stating that in order to earn the credibility required to add value at a strategic level, you need to ensure that the trains run on time every day. Running the IT factory so that services are consistently delivered on time, on value, and on budget is not very sexy. It is, however, an imperative; it is job one for a CIO.

Lessons Learned

In this chapter we have compared and contrasted the concepts of leadership and management. We have also defined some of the key roles that effective leaders must play in transforming their organizations. Let's recap what we've learned:

- Leadership and management are different sets of muscles.
- Leadership focuses on helping people understand where the team is going and why the stated destination has been chosen.
- Management helps people figure out how to chart the course to arrive at the stated destination.
- Transformational leaders are required to play many roles. These include:
  - Business executive—helping drive business outcomes such as revenue creation and expansion, process re-engineering, and cost efficiency for the organization

- Evangelist—inspiring your people and getting them fired up about the journey you are about to embark upon
- Captain of the ship—charting the course for success
- Teacher and coach—providing people the skills and tools they require to successfully complete the journey
- Cheerleader—pumping people up and keeping them motivated even when challenges occur and success is not in sight
- Strategist—developing the strategies required to complete the mission
- Innovator—working with people to think outside the box and develop novel approaches to addressing the challenges that stand between you and your objectives
- Shop foreman—the unglamorous but critical role of running the utility and keeping the lights on while you climb the value chain

CHAPTER 2

That Vision Thing

This chapter will focus on the role that organizational vision plays in ensuring a successful transformation. Specifically, we will focus on the following concepts:

- ☐ Learning the importance of an effective vision
- ☐ Determining whose vision it is
- ☐ Ensuring that employees feel a sense of ownership for the vision
- ☐ Learning the effective way to create a vision
- ☐ Aligning the vision with people's personal visions
- ☐ Inspiring people through the use of the vision
- ☐ Looking at ways to make the vision real in people's daily lives

Importance of Vision

Over the years, I have heard a lot about the concept of vision. I have personally been involved in the creation of the vision statement for a number of large, complex organizations. From this experience, I learned a great deal about the right and wrong way to develop and articulate an organization's vision. Before we venture into a discussion about how to do the *vision thing,* let's take a moment to discuss why it is so important.

All of us work, for many reasons. At the bottom of Maslow's hierarchy of needs pyramid is the need to feed our families and ourselves, put a roof over our heads, and pay the countless other bills we have each month.[1] Although fear of hunger and homelessness is certainly a great motivator, that only gets you so far. To truly tap into the full passion, talent, and effort of a human being, you must appeal to something higher than basic needs. Vision is, first of all, a call to that higher meaning. A good vision should touch a part of individuals that makes them aspire to give their best and be their best. A good organizational vision is also a rallying cry—a call to arms, if you will. It should be a higher calling that crystallizes the purpose of the organization in the minds of its stakeholders and binds them together to achieve a common purpose that resonates with them at a deeper level. A good vision is also an excellent way to articulate the purpose and meaning of an organization to the outside world so that they understand what makes the organization tick.

Although all of these issues are important, I feel the reason vision is so important is that it creates a picture of a future state that people can get excited about. When they know the vision, they can rally around it and be willing to commit themselves fully to accomplishing the goals.

Deciding Whose Vision It Is

I have witnessed organizations make several mistakes in the crafting of their vision. Perhaps the most egregious mistake organizations make works like this. The top leaders in an organization decide they need to create a new vision. This small group of individuals sequesters themselves in some five-star hotel, resort, or conference

---

[1] Abraham Maslow's hierarchy of needs was first published in his article, "A Theory of Human Motivation," *Psychological Review* 50(4) (1943):370–396.

room for some extended period of time to hammer out the new vision. Lots of dialogue, political maneuvering, energy, and compromising follow. After what seems like an eternity to the participants, a final document is created that expresses the new vision. This reminds me of Mel Brooks's classic movie *History of the World,* where Moses carries down the 15 (oops! I dropped a tablet!) Ten Commandments from the mountain and gives them to the people. In a similar fashion, the CEO calls a town hall meeting to unveil the new vision and to tell people, "This is our new vision. You will cherish it, be motivated by it, and abide by it." Does this sound familiar to you? Have you seen this movie? Why doesn't this work?

Through the Lens of the CIO—Is the Organization's Vision Your Vision?

I remember a number of years ago taking my girls to the circus. We sat next to a young family with a little boy about five years old who was crying and wanted no part of the experience! I chatted with his father, who was visibly upset by the situation. He stated that he had put a lot of time and effort into planning this event for his child and had also spent his hard-earned money to pay for good seats so that his kid could see the clowns up close and personal. Me being me, I couldn't help asking the little boy what was upsetting him so. He said to me, "I hate clowns! They scare me!"

This little story reminds me so much of how most CIOs go through the process of developing and articulating a vision. They come up with a vision that really resonates with them and gets them motivated and excited. They go through this process in a virtual vacuum. Then they seem perplexed when their people aren't jumping up and down with excitement upon being provided this new direction.

I remember being part of a large IT organization that went through a major overhaul. It was termed a "transformation" effort

(continued)

(Continued)

(we were even given T-shirts with a picture of a butterfly on it!). I was one of the lucky chosen ones from the rank and file who were selected to be part of the vision-creation process. A highly paid outside consulting firm was brought in to develop a new vision and organizational alignment. The people in the organization were never told why this was taking place. They feared the consultants and viewed them as a threat to their jobs. They didn't trust their management, who they felt was out of touch with the realities and challenges they were dealing with day in and day out. A small cadre of people (myself included) were sequestered for long periods of time to come up with a new vision and strategy, and the only communication with the majority of the staff were some high-level fluff e-mails telling them how great things were going.

When all was said and done, the "transformation" was unveiled. Our clients, who at best were kept at arm's length from this process, viewed this as the "flavor of the day" and went back to business as usual. Many of our people were either downsized or put into new and uncomfortable roles, and the ones who remained in the company were not drinking the Kool-Aid! Some progress was made and some things did get better, but three years after the effort was completed, it was still a suboptimal situation.

I remember asking one particular teammate what he thought about the new vision. His comment was, "This isn't my vision—it's theirs!" When you undertake to develop and launch a new vision, it's critical to ask yourself: "Whose vision is it, anyway?"

Helping Employees Feel Ownership

There is one minor problem with this approach to creating and implementing a vision. The only people who buy into it (if you are lucky!) are those who helped create it. For the rest of the organization, this is simply another edict being foisted onto them by the bigwigs. They have no personal connection to this vision, no emotional attachment to it, and no reason to buy into it on a visceral level. This is simply one more thing taking them away from being productive and getting their jobs done. What is missing here is a sense of ownership. No one has taken the time and effort to engage the people in the process of developing the vision. There is no personal buy-in. People don't understand how or why they should connect to the vision and what it means to them on a day-in, day-out basis. Bottom line, there is no sense of ownership on a personal level for making the vision a reality.

Creating the Vision

Although it might be challenging if not impossible to have every single member of an organization actively participate in the creation of a vision, it is imperative that each person feels that he or she had input into the process and sees and feels something that matters *personally* in the vision. One of the ways I have seen this accomplished is by having representatives of the different groups that make up an organization participate in the process of defining the vision.

In the process of developing the vision, the way these representatives are chosen is critical. The organization shouldn't simply select the managers of each of the functional groups. Instead, they should select a diverse group from among the informal leaders from each of the groups. In order to ensure that you have chosen the right people, you need to answer a few questions. Who has the most influence with this group? Who do people seem to rally around or hang out with? Who do people go to with their questions and concerns? Who has the answers when people have questions or concerns? Many times, the real leader in a group is not the person with the most formal authority or the loftiest title. Find the real leader and invite that person to participate in the creation of the vision.

You must also provide people the time and space from their normal responsibilities to invest in developing the vision. If you ask employees to be a part of this effort without taking into consideration the impact this time and effort will have on their daily work, they are more likely to view their involvement in this process as a negative thing, with negative consequences to their work. You also need to ensure that there is a conduit for these informal leaders to be able to share with their group the things they are doing and the progress being made on the creation of the vision.

Aligning Your Vision with the Vision of Your People

Once a vision is created, a leader must take the time and effort to align his or her people behind it. This requires time and energy to communicate the vision, answer people's questions, explain the importance of the vision, and help people understand how the vision impacts them and, more importantly, how what they do impacts the organization's ability to accomplish the vision. People must feel inspired by the vision and see a connection between their roles and their beliefs and the accomplishment of the vision. In order to accomplish this, you must first understand what makes a person tick. I have been fortunate enough to lead a number of teams over the course of my career. Many of these teams went on to accomplish wonderful things (for which I take little credit!). I was once asked by an interviewer how I lead people. My response was that I didn't lead people—I led *persons*. This is not a matter of semantics but, rather, an important way of thinking of leadership. Each person is a unique combination of talents, hopes, dreams, experiences, and desires. The idea that a one-size-fits-all approach to motivating people will do the trick is simply a lazy approach to trying to find a shortcut to leadership. Each person on your team is wired differently, so it is imperative that you take the time and effort to understand your team members as individuals and to reach out to help them relate to the vision in a way that resonates with them. Unless you do this, you can never fully get them to buy into the vision with their hearts and souls.

Through the Lens of the CIO—What if You Have No Clear Organizational Direction?

Have you ever worked for an organization that didn't have a clear vision? I have had the interesting experience of working for leaders who couldn't tell me what we were focused on accomplishing or why! Our IT organization was not aligned with the corporate direction. We were viewed as a utility, and many times, not even a good one!

All of us at one time or another have worked for poor leaders who were unable to articulate a real vision of what success looked like or how the work we performed as an organization mapped to the bottom-line outcomes of the firms we were a part of. We've all worked for people who were terrible communicators and who couldn't lead their way out of a paper bag. I once had a colleague who was struggling with his manager say to me, "I give up! I can't get a straight answer from my boss. He's a clown! He doesn't get it or doesn't seem to care, so why should I?" After completing his tirade, he asked for my opinion on how he should proceed. I told him, "Just because you work for a clown doesn't give you license to join the circus!"

Anyone who has worked for me will tell you that one message I repeat ad nauseam is that leadership begins with me. Regardless of who you are, what role you play in the organization, and what your scope of impact, you can always control how you play the game. It's very easy to throw your hands up in disgust

(continued)

(*Continued*)

and settle on being mediocre. In some organizations, this may not even be noticed. But beware of this course of action, as an insidious thing can happen. Mediocrity can creep into your bloodstream. All of a sudden, you become one of "them." Instead of being part of the solution, you have now devolved into being part of the problem. You can rationalize and justify this approach a million ways to Sunday, but the bottom line is that at the end of the day you as a professional are the one who will suffer.

If you find yourself in this situation, there are two constructive things you can do. The first is to leave! Get out and run away as fast as you can. If you are truly working in a poisonous environment, it might be time to change the scenery. But what if you don't want to, or—given the realities of the economic climate or the job market—what if you can't move on to another opportunity? Then you be the change you want to see. You set the course for your people that your management is ill equipped to set for you. You be the beacon in a world of darkness. Funny thing happens when you take this approach. First of all, you and your people feel a whole lot better about life! Second, sometimes the people above you in the food chain start to take notice. They wonder what's going on in this area. Why are clients starting to flock to these people? What are they doing that the rest of us aren't? Someone may even be bold enough to try to figure out what's happening here and whether it can be emulated in other parts of the organization. Be careful: You may start something that impacts the dysfunction!

Inspiring Others to Share the Vision

This next concept may make you feel a bit uncomfortable. I know it was tough for me to embrace at first. I went to a conference once where one of the presenters asked the question, "Do you inspire your people?" I initially balked at this notion. After all, "inspiration" was best left to people of great integrity and spirituality. It was also the stuff of great movements. Martin Luther King Jr. inspired people. How was some IT executive supposed to inspire people? I struggled with this concept for a long time until I finally wrapped my brain around the fact that leadership on any level in any field of endeavor did indeed require a level of inspiration in order to create great results.

I remember an old story I once heard about a man who was walking past a construction site. He walked up to the first laborer and asked what he was doing. The mason shared that he was "making twenty bucks an hour laying bricks." This didn't satisfy the man's curiosity, so he asked the same question to another laborer. The second worker shared that he was "building the greatest cathedral in the world." Both workers had the same job, but the second worker had a greater vision. This was due to a higher level of inspiration. What do your people feel they are doing? Have you asked them? Are they simply making a living, or are they building a life? Are they a part of a greater purpose that they are proud of, or are they simply cogs in a machine?

Making the Vision Real for People

In order to make a vision real for people, they must feel a part of the movement. As a leader, it is imperative that you work with people to help them understand the vision, feel a connection to the vision, and feel a real sense of ownership for the attainment of the vision. Perhaps the most important thing you can do to accomplish these objectives is to help incorporate the vision in a person's daily life.

This has two aspects. The first is to work with individuals to craft their objectives and deliverables in such a way as to have a connection to the overarching objectives associated with the vision. Let's look at an example. If part of the vision is to drive new revenue opportunities, you must help the person understand how what they do on a daily basis supports this objective, either directly by driving revenue or indirectly by supporting the people responsible for driving revenue. The other thing you must do is make the person feel a part of the larger team and a part of achieving the vision. One approach I have used is to have key executives at my staff meeting to explain what they do, how it ties to the vision, and how the work my team performs supports them in this endeavor. This has a number of positive benefits. It helps educate my team on what these leaders are focused on. It helps them see a connection between the work they do and the achievement of the leaders' objectives. Perhaps most importantly, it makes people feel a personal connection to the leader and the vision on an emotional level.

Lessons Learned

- Having a compelling vision that inspires your team is a critical part of any transformation effort.
- It is imperative that the members of the team feel that they have been a key part of developing the vision.
- People must feel a sense of ownership and accountability for the vision.
- There is a right and wrong way to develop a vision. Having people engaged in every part of the process is the right way.
- For a vision to be effective, people must see themselves, their daily efforts, and their personal vision as closely aligned to the organization's vision.
- For a vision to be effective, it must inspire people to perform at their optimal level.
- An effective vision is a real vision that people can embrace.

CHAPTER 3

It's the Business, Stupid!

This chapter will focus on the only reason anyone truly cares about information technology—the ability to leverage information and technology to drive business value! Specifically, we will focus on the following concepts:

- Describing the real purpose of IT within a business
- Evaluating IT–business alignment
- Considering three questions as they relate to the mission of your organization.
- Taking a look at fiscal management and leveraging IT as an investment instead of a cost.
- Finding ways that IT can actually help drive top-line revenue.
- Discussing CIO effectiveness in engaging the board of directors.
- Examining the most important role a CIO plays—business leader.
- Discussing the type of metrics that matter to most business executives.
- Learning to focus on what matters most to your key stakeholders.
- Understanding how perception really is reality!

Many of us remember Bill Clinton's 1992 presidential campaign. In Clinton's Arkansas campaign headquarters, Campaign

Manager James Carville had a list of three key points—the most memorable being, "The economy, stupid."[1] Although this might seem trite, it is important to understand the crystallizing impact of this statement. The Clinton campaign's ability to focus people on this message and leverage it as a rallying cry led to what many considered to be a surprising victory in that election.

As a CIO, I have been exposed to many technologists who have a great deal of angst regarding the fact that their management or board of directors doesn't understand what they do or how important technology and information are to the mission of the organization. Whenever I come across this concern, I ask a question along the following lines. Say your company was going to relocate you to Spain. Would you expect the entire population of Spain to become fluent in English just so they could communicate with you? Of course not! It would be incumbent upon you to learn to speak Spanish in order to function in their world. Why is it, then, that some technology leaders feel that business leaders should learn to speak "geek" instead of taking responsibility for being able to speak the language of business? Business leaders are responsible for driving business results. As an IT executive, you are expected to be a business leader. This means speaking the language of business and being comfortable in the world of business.

The Purpose of IT

Let me start by admitting that I am not your prototypical IT person. I am not enamored with technology for technology's sake. I don't run out to buy the next exciting new gadget the day it

---

[1] Richard Alleyne, "Gordon Brown: It's the economy, stupid!" *The Daily Telegraph*. May 23, 2008. Accessed at web.archive.org/web/20080526075655/http://www.telegraph.co.uk/news/newstopics/by_election_crewe_and_nantwich/2015038/Gordon-Brown-It%27s-the-economy,-stupid!.html.

comes out. I did not build Heathkits as a kid (as a matter of fact, the model cars I built always wound up having "spare" parts!). I am not naturally technically inclined. I received the same SAT score on the math portion as I did on the language portion (650 on each, for those of you who care). My right brain works as well (or as poorly, depending on who you ask!) as my left brain. I come at IT from a little different angle than some IT executives. To me, technology and information have only one real purpose—that is, to promote the business objectives of the organization. I love it when people start talking about service level agreements (SLAs) with "five nines." The only SLA I have ever seen that mattered was whether the leadership of an organization thought that they were gleaning business value from the investment they made in IT. Providing value to the organization is the primary purpose of information technology; everything else is secondary.

The Foolishness of Alignment

Over the past few years, virtually every trade journal I have read and almost every conference I have attended has focused on IT–business alignment. I have a very visceral reaction to this topic. I think it's a bunch of hooey (I believe that is a more politically correct term to use than what originally came to mind!). My disgust with this term is not due to my lack of belief that IT should be on the same page as business. Rather my negative reaction is exactly because of this belief! Let me explain.

My understanding of the word *alignment* (and granted, I'm not the sharpest tool in the shed!) is the bringing together of two separate things so that they converge on a common purpose. To be a proponent of IT–business alignment (and notice how technologists usually put the IT portion first!) is to suggest that IT is somehow something separate from the business. If this is the case, why don't we talk about finance–business alignment? How about marketing–business alignment? The answer is obvious: It's because finance and marketing are not separate from the business—they are **part of** the business! I would argue, so is IT! No IT organization (unless you are talking about an IT capability at a technology company) is a standalone entity. IT is part of the enterprise it supports in the same ways as these other functional entities. Does your CFO have a plan to "align" with the CEO? If he's not already in alignment, he might be on his way to unemployment! Using this terminology and thought process creates an artificial barrier between IT and the rest of "business" when, in reality, IT is a crucial part of any business.

Three Questions about IT's Role in the Organization's Mission

Being of Italian descent, I have been taught that things come in threes! I guess that includes questions! As a leader of a functional entity (i.e., IT), you should ask yourself three questions on an ongoing basis:

1. *What outcomes are we striving for?* What are the major objectives of the organization? What goals must we reach in order to further our mission? What is core to accomplishing our vision? What are the things that matter and will make a difference to the success and long-term viability of the enterprise?
2. *How do the efforts of my organization help us achieve these outcomes?* How do the day-to-day activities performed in my area contribute to our success? Are we supporting revenue generation? Are we attracting more customers? Are we driving operational efficiencies? Are we improving key business processes (e.g., customer service, manufacturing)?
3. *If our focus and objectives are not supporting these key imperatives, then why are we doing them?*

I am reminded of the story of the Easter ham. A little girl asked, "Mommy, why do you cut the ends off the Easter ham before you cook it?" Her mother pondered this question and said, "Sweetheart, I really don't know. Grandma always did it that way; why don't you ask her?" The little girl proceeded to ask her grandmother the same question. Her response was similar to her daughter's: "I don't know . . . my mom always did it that way." Finally, the little girl asked her 90-year-old great-grandmother. "Nana, why did you cut the ends off the Easter ham before you cooked it?" The old woman pondered the question and then replied, "Well, honey, my roasting pan was too small to fit a large ham, so I had to slice off the ends before I put the ham in the oven." I am reminded of this little vignette every time I hear someone say, "We've always done it that way." My response is . . . so what? You need to challenge your assumptions and actions all the time and not just do things because you always have!

Fiscal Management—IT Is an Investment, Not a Cost

It amazes me how many IT executives view the CFO as their enemy and moan and groan about having to budget and manage to a budget. Can you imagine another business executive complaining about the financial portion of the job? Managing the finances is a crucial part of any executive's responsibility. Every leader must live within a set of fiscal constraints (except for the federal government, and we all have seen where that has led!). Fiduciary responsibility is "table stakes" for any executive.

The key to handling the financial aspect of the job is viewing (and making sure your board views) IT as an investment, not a cost. This is not semantics or smoke and mirrors! A cost suggests something that is "sunk." You pay a sum of money and you get something in return once. An investment is something that yields dividends. Those dividends might represent additional revenue, cost savings, improvements in customer satisfaction, process changes, and so on. The idea of IT as a cost of doing business is a killer for a CIO. You quickly must get your board and executive team to view IT as an investment that pays dividends and is a capability to be leveraged.

Many times I will hear of IT executives "playing games" with their budgets. This is akin to keeping two sets of books! As a leader, you should manage your budget like it's your own money—because as a leader in your organization, it is! As a key stakeholder in the health of your organization, you need to understand that every penny you spend is a penny that can't be invested in sales, marketing, advertising, or research and development. Does this mean you shouldn't spend the money? Not necessarily. What it does mean is that you need to decide to spend that money knowing the impact it will have and knowing that there isn't a limitless pot of gold at the end of the proverbial rainbow!

Whenever you request funding, you need to be able to articulate the expected return on that investment. I don't necessarily mean this in the financial definition's sense of the word (although that is a great place to start!). I mean you need to articulate what your leadership should expect to be different because you have invested this money and how that will impact the business. I have also found that it is easier for the heads of your business units to get funding than it is for a CIO. You should always partner with your business unit executives to ensure that the projects being proposed are of great value to them, that the projects have a direct business impact, that the business leaders are willing to get in front of the board and sponsor these initiatives, and that they share accountability for ensuring that the projects succeed and return value for the investment. The credibility of having a business owner state the importance and the need for a project cannot be underestimated.

IT as a Tool to Drive Revenue

Many CIOs are focused on the cost side of the financial equation. For most IT organizations, containing costs is the primary focus when it comes to their financial contribution to their companies. However, in these challenging economic times, that is not enough.

Technology and information provide a number of opportunities to help directly and indirectly drive new revenue and enhance existing revenue streams. One of the most obvious opportunities is to be able to sell your products and services online. Most people today conduct a large portion of their purchases online—whether that be books, music, clothing, or even tickets to sports and entertainment events. Another obvious opportunity is to leverage social media to help get your marketing messaging in the public's eye. But there are also less obvious opportunities.

In my current role, we were able to leverage existing wireless networking technologies to, in essence, expand the footprint of our point-of-sales capabilities. Therefore, standalone kiosks that previously had only been able to take cash tender were expanded to accept credit and debit card transactions. As you can imagine, this had a significant positive impact on food and concession revenue. Another thing we leveraged was access security. Most events have a limit to how many fans they can accommodate before running the risk of having a public safety issue. However, by knowing real time how many people are on site, you now have the opportunity to extend the sales of tickets to additional fans for opportunities such as grounds passes or for standing-room only. In our case, this significantly increased ticket revenue. Another example is developing a novel technology solution that can be leveraged by other companies in your industry. We are actually working on licensing a solution we developed in house that other sports and entertainment events can leverage for security and event operations. These examples come from my world, but in every industry there are opportunities that simply take a keen eye and a bit of creativity. In many cases, the additional investment is negligible but the financial impact, as well as the business goodwill this creates, can be substantial. Do you want to be seen as a business leader? Do you want to have a great relationship with your CEO, CFO, and board of directors? One surefire way to accomplish this is by being seen as someone who helps to feed the revenue engine.

Ways to Engage the Board

One of the responsibilities of a CIO that strikes terror into the hearts of many IT executives is presenting to, and engaging with, the board of directors. For someone who is new to this dynamic, this can be a daunting task. While only the individual can overcome her "stage fright," I can make some suggestions that can help create a more positive experience in the boardroom.

My first suggestion is that a CIO should stand out in the boardroom by *not* standing out in the boardroom! Is that confusing enough for you? What I mean by this is quite simple. The people who engage with the board, as well as the members of the board themselves, are usually accomplished businesspeople. They speak the language of business and expect to discuss business-related topics. As an executive of the organization, so must you! If you come into the room speaking *geek* (i.e., using three-letter acronyms talking about VPNs and SOA), not only will the board not understand you but also they will not take you or your message seriously. However, if you present to the board your plans and efforts to drive revenue, improve shareholder value, and lower the cost structure of running your operations, they will both understand you and take interest in your message. When engaging the board, it is critical that you accomplish three major objectives:

1. *Create an atmosphere of confidence* Board-level people expect to engage with individuals who are confident in their value and in delivering their messages. I remember an old commercial for an antiperspirant with the tagline "Never let them see you sweat!" This is a very important dynamic. There is an old expression that dogs can smell fear. The worst thing you can do is portray an image of someone who is intimidated to be in the situation. How can you avoid this? Remember why you are there in the first place. You are a subject matter expert, and you bring a level of acumen and value in an area that is of importance and significance to the organization. You have an important message to deliver, and you are psyched to deliver it! This leads to your next objective.

2. *Exude passion* People remember great speakers not so much because of how eloquent they are (although that never hurts!) but because of their passion about their message. Are you excited about what you have to share with the board? Is it important to them and to the organization? Do you feel a sense of pride and energy about your message? One of the things I've learned in my career is that people buy into the messenger before they buy into the message! If you have passion about your message and a sense of enthusiasm about how you carry out your work, you can get people excited about selling ice in Alaska! If you are not enthusiastic about your message, you won't even get a child excited about a trip to Disney World! I am not suggesting a manic, over-the-top kind of passion, but rather, an honest level of energy that is evident in your walk, your speech, your gestures, and your mannerisms. In delivering a message, you are taking people on a journey. Make sure that they feel it's a journey filled with excitement and promise, not a trip to the dentist!

3. *Create a connection* This happens not only in the boardroom but also before and after your experience there. It can be easy to be intimidated by the board. After all, they are usually very successful people and you may feel that you need them a lot more than they need you! But at the end of the day, they are people just like you and me. Make an effort to get to know them as people. I am not suggesting some false level of interest or a disingenuous approach to "shaking hands and kissing babies." I mean taking a genuine interest in them as people and developing relationships. Some of the most interesting, intelligent, successful, and nicest people I have ever met have been members of my board of directors. I have been blessed to have the opportunity to learn from them as businesspeople and get to know them as human beings. I have enjoyed getting to learn more about their interests and ambitions, as well as their motivation for serving on our board. When I walk into the boardroom, they know that I am genuinely happy to see them. I also feel that they are happy to see me! This is a process that needs to be nurtured over time. But even the neophyte can make an effort to learn more about his board members prior to presenting to them and to work on making a connection with them when delivering his message. People are people. They care about people who care about them. They are interested in people who are interested in them. They support people who support their efforts. There are no shortcuts here—just real caring and connection.

Through the Lens of the CIO—Can You Spot the CIO in the Boardroom?

You hear a lot of conversation these days about the roles CIOs do and should play in engaging with their board of directors. CIOs grind their teeth in frustration about their perceived lack of visibility and engagement with their boards. They think that they don't always have the opportunity to get their message across and that most members of their boards don't really understand or appreciate the value that they bring to the table. There is a lack of clarity regarding their role in partnering with the governance of their organization.

I'd like to have you play a bit of a virtual game that I like to call "Can you spot the CIO?" Here's how it works. You are a stranger to an organization and do not know the cast of characters. You get to sit behind a transparent glass window and can see and hear all of the individuals at the company's board meeting. The agenda is passed out and the meeting begins. Based on what people are saying and how they are reacting to the issues at hand, can you single out the CIO?

Most of the time, it's (unfortunately) pretty easy to spot the CIO. He is the person who seems ill at ease in the room. If you watch the human dynamics at play, he is the lone ranger who is not engaged in the friendly banter with the other people in the room. He is often quiet during the business conversation and does not add a lot of value or input into discussions regarding how to invest the company's resources, what strategy to pursue, or what the organization's future objectives should be. Occasionally, he is called on to weigh in on tactical issues. When he does, he talks in "geek speak," mentioning VPNs and lifecycle management and other terms that the other people in the room clearly do not understand. He gets frustrated because the others don't seem to "get it" when he explains the intricacies of the latest system rollout.

My premise is that an effective CIO can't be easily identified if you are playing this game. She is first and foremost a business leader, so her conversation tends to focus on business outcomes and be communicated in business and financial terms. She is weighing in on all aspects of the business, because as a leader, she has the ability to impact all aspects of the business. She also has a broad perspective across the entire enterprise as to how

(*continued*)

(*Continued*)

things work from both a process and a human dynamics perspective. She understands who is working with whom, why, and how it all comes together. Other than the CEO, probably no one else at the executive level has as varied and holistic a view of the entire organization. Therefore, she understands that she has a responsibility to bring issues and opportunities to light and to provide a unique perspective on how the organization can leverage both technology as well as information to make better decisions and drive better outcomes.

If I peeked into your boardroom, what would I see? Would I be able to spot you immediately, or would I not be able to tell you from any other senior executive? Interesting game, don't you think?

The CIO as a Business Leader, Not Technologist

By now, hopefully you have gotten the message that your role is to be a business leader, not a "propeller-head"! Even the most savvy and experienced CIOs can fall into traps and ruts along the way. In order to avoid this, I suggest a little exercise that you should perform on an ongoing basis. Ask and answer the following three simple questions:

1. *Who are you talking to?* This is a very basic litmus test. There are several groups of people you should engage with on a regular basis. You should be speaking with:
   - External consumers of your organization's services or products
   - Internal clients of your services
   - Your staff
   - Your key partners and vendors
   - Your key business unit executives
   - Your management

- Your board of directors
- Your peers in the industry and other subject matter experts

It's very easy to get caught up spending all of your time with the one or two groups that you feel most comfortable with. For many people, that is usually members of your own staff. While it is important to spend some inward-facing time, this needs to be one small piece of the puzzle.

2. *What are you talking about?* The kind of leader you are is easily evidenced by what you are focused on. Are you focused on mission-related objectives such as driving new revenue, acquiring new customers, improving business processes, or rationalizing costs? These are the areas of focus for business leaders. By contrast, do you spend most of your time discussing issues of reliability, availability, integration, or technology implementation? If so, your focus is on being more of a technology leader. Please understand that in no way do I mean to express this in the form of a value judgment! There is nothing wrong with being a technology leader. We absolutely need quality technical leaders to ensure we can provide the services required to run our businesses. These people play a vitally important role. Only you can decide what you aspire to and how you want to add value. Just understand the differences and make a conscious decision to talk the talk of the world you aspire to live in.

3. *What language are you speaking?* This goes hand in glove with the previous question. A business executive speaks the language of business. She talks about mission-related topics and issues that are salient to her organization's overarching objectives and focus. She discusses a project's return on investment and how the outcomes will create new revenue streams or drive cost efficiencies. A technologist speaks the language of technology—SLAs, VPNs, SaaS, SOA, M-O-U-S-E! You get the picture!

I am always stunned when CIOs get frustrated that their board members and fellow executives don't speak in acronyms. Once you are in the boardroom, you are now in their country. Therefore, it is incumbent upon you to learn to speak their language, not for them to speak yours.

Meaningful Metrics

IT leaders, more than any other functional group I know of, are extremely focused on metrics. There is an old adage that states you can't manage what you can't measure. I am a believer in metrics as well. However, my version of metrics is somewhat different from what most technology executives focus on.

If you speak to most IT executives about metrics, you will hear a lot about "nines." While three sixes is the language of Lucifer, five nines seems to be the language of IT. There is a lot of talk about systems availability and network availability and reports that show we are at 99.97 percent of something or other. Now don't get me wrong: Availability of critical services and systems is absolutely imperative. However if you start talking to your CEO about these metrics, he might go into a semiconscious state of being.

Business leaders and executives care about metrics as well. But their metrics focus on issues such as revenue creation, cost avoidance, project ROI, opportunity costs, and so on. See the difference? Once again, it is our responsibility to speak a language that resonates with our audience. That language is the language of business and finance.

Focus on What Matters

Very few leaders are bored in their roles. There are more issues and opportunities than there are hours available in the day. I hear a lot of people complain that they would be more effective if they just had more time. The last time I checked, all of us, regardless of who we are, have 24 hours in a day. The key, therefore, is not to find more time, but to better leverage the allotment of time we are all given.

There is an old adage that says the good is the enemy of the great. Let's talk about this a bit. When I first took on my current role, there were more opportunities for improvement (i.e., train wrecks) than I could possibly address. There were two challenges associated with addressing the situation. The first was prioritization. When everything is broken, it can feel overwhelming. The emotional reaction is to run around plugging up holes in the dike. The problem with that approach is that you run out of fingers pretty quickly. You have to take a step backward, think about and devote your efforts to what really matters. In every organization, there is a short list of things that will make the difference between success and failure. There are items that are so critical that failure to address them will jeopardize the entire endeavor. There are also opportunities so important and so fleeting that they can be game changers. Failure to seize strategic opportunities or address critical exposures can be the difference between winning and losing the game.

When deciding how to invest your time and effort (as well as your budgets), you need to focus on those high-priority opportunities and problems that really matter. This is easier said than done. Personally, it was extremely difficult for me to focus my efforts on a few major items at a time when all around me I could see and feel other issues that warranted my attention. However, the surest way to lose a war is to try to fight too many battles on too many fronts at the same time. Although multitasking is all the rage these days, and is a necessary reality in our lives, it is vital to invest focus and energy on a few critical items, even at the expense of others. If your house was on fire, would you grab your family and run out or would you worry about the dishwasher not working? If the fire is quickly contained, you will eventually need to fix the dishwasher, but if the house burns to the ground, you won't have to worry about it, will you? As a leader, you need to marshal your limited troops and resources to win the battles that allow you to fight another day. At a later time, you can fix the less critical problems.

Through the Lens of the CIO – I Finally Got a Seat at the Table! Now What?

You can't read a trade journal or attend an IT conference without someone talking about the need for the CIO to have "a seat at the table." There is great frustration about the inability of the CIO to have regular and visible engagement with the board of directors. I understand this frustration very well. However, I would propose to you that there might be something worse for some CIOs than not having a seat at the table. That worse scenario could be actually having a seat at the table!

When I was a young child, I was often chosen to represent my class or my school in local spelling bees. This was viewed by my teachers as a wonderful educational opportunity. For me at the time, it was a fate worse than death! I was painfully shy and avoided bringing attention to myself like the plague. I would purposely misspell a word fairly early in the contest in order to get off the stage. My teachers were perplexed by my poor performance when they knew I was a better speller than that! At the age of 15, I joined a rock band and performed live for the first time. I was doing my best to hide behind my amplifier and hoping no one would notice me. At one point in the set, I was called upon to sing a song that no one else had the vocal range to sing. I dreaded this moment. I finally started singing the song, and I noticed something. People seemed to be enjoying my performance. I was actually good at something! I quickly became comfortable sharing this talent with others. I started to pull my weight with the band and leverage my talent to help improve our performances.

When you are "at the table," you are expected to contribute. You are not expected to be a bump on a log. I've known CIOs who were panic-stricken because after years of lobbying for a seat at the table, they had been invited into the inner sanctum! As the old phrase goes, be careful what you wish for! Now that they were expected to participate, they had no idea how or what to contribute to the proceedings. I have coached IT executives and prepared them for this new opportunity by helping them focus on developing relationships with the people at the table as well as fully understanding the business issues at hand so that they could make a meaningful contribution to the conversation.

If you were invited into the boardroom tomorrow, would you be comfortable or terrified? Are you familiar enough with what your organization is trying to accomplish in terms of your core business to add value to this dialogue? Or are you a one-trick pony who knows a few technical things that you have trouble explaining to a nontechnical audience and who wouldn't have any other value to add to the rest of the conversation? What are you doing to prepare yourself to be seen as a business leader, as opposed to a technical expert?

Managing Perception versus Reality

I have told my team many times (to the point that they are sick of hearing it) that perception is reality. It doesn't matter what the facts are if the people in question perceive it to be something else. This is a double-edged sword that can work for you or against you.

I have seen CIOs argue with their clients regarding satisfaction with their services. They will pull out reports and quote SLA metrics (we've talked about metrics before) and try to convince their clients that things are better than they feel they are. This is a fruitless exercise because perception is a far stronger emotional tug than facts. I have also seen this work for my benefit. When we conducted our first IT scorecard survey, we got (justifiably) slammed for all the problems we were experiencing. Projects were notorious for coming in late and over budget. IT was terrible at communicating with our clients. The community felt that we were not responsive to their issues and concerns and our services were deemed unreliable. As the old joke goes, "Other than that, Mrs. Lincoln, how was the play?" The scores we received (on a scale of 1 to 5, where 1 is awful and 5 is outstanding) were in the high 2s and low 3s. Six months later when we administered our second scorecard survey, the scores had gone up to the high 3s and low 4s! Now don't get me wrong, we had made some important progress in starting to address key issues. But we were still very much a work in progress with much room for improvement. Why such an uptick on the scores? Well, the clients' perception was that things were getting better. IT was communicating with them. We were taking their issues seriously and exhibiting a focus and a sense of urgency that had been missing in the past. Had we really gotten that much better in six months? Honestly . . . no. But the perception of the team had improved that much.

Lessons Learned

- The only real value that IT has within an organization is the ability to drive business value and help accomplish business results.
- Alignment is a ridiculous concept! IT should not aspire to align with the business because it is a part of the business! The real aim should be for IT to be perceived as a critical core component to driving your business strategy.
- CIOs should constantly challenge themselves to ensure that the things their organization is focused on are

helping to drive the strategic imperatives of the company. CIOs should ensure that all of the IT organization's resources—both human and financial—are focused on the things that matter most to the business.

- Fiscal management is the fiduciary responsibility of every business executive, including the CIO. The CIO should spend and invest the company's money as if it were his own!
- If applied effectively, IT can be an investment to be leveraged, as opposed to a cost of doing business.
- IT can and should focus on innovative ways to help the organization drive top-line revenue by developing new revenue streams and helping to expand existing revenue streams.
- A CIO must learn how to effectively engage with the members of the board and develop the ability to blend in and be viewed as a business executive instead of a technical expert.
- The most important role a CIO plays is the role of business executive and leader. CIOs must develop a grasp of the company's business and apply their business acumen as well as their technical expertise to all matters.
- The only metrics that matter are the metrics that businesses use to track success. Technical metrics are only important as they apply to driving business results.
- CIOs have a myriad of things to which they can devote money and resources. It is critical to identify and focus on only the items that will have the most critical impact to the business.
- As in every other aspect of life, perception is reality. A CIO must effectively deal with and improve the perception that the organization has about IT and about the CIO as a business leader.

CHAPTER 4

Communication

In this chapter we will focus on communication. Specifically, we will focus on the following concepts:

- ☐ Explaining the importance that effective communication has in impacting CIO success
- ☐ Listening as opposed to talking
- ☐ Determining who is the CIO's target audience for communicating with
- ☐ Communicating in the best way with this audience
- ☐ Engaging target audiences and how frequently CIOs should do so
- ☐ Effectively marketing as a CIO
- ☐ Personal branding in conveying a compelling message
- ☐ Examining the nuances of communicating with a volunteer army
- ☐ Focusing on the issue, not the person
- ☐ Reviewing the importance of honesty and transparency

The Importance of Communication

Of all the skills a leader must possess, one of the most important is the ability to effectively communicate with people. I have met a number of leaders in my day who felt very uncomfortable in this capacity. They felt that in order to effectively communicate, they needed to be great orators like Cicero or inspirational motivators like Knute Rockne. Although these are certainly wonderful qualities to possess, they are not prerequisites to effective communication. The most important aspect of being a good communicator is being authentic. The most important aspect in communicating is to "say what you mean and mean what you say." People need to be able to trust what you communicate to them. They must also know that your words are backed up by genuine feelings and actions. There must always be congruence between your words and your actions. As the old saying goes, "What you do speaks so loud I can't hear what you say!" Great communicators are able to get their message across not because of the words they use but because of their ability to connect with people. You must have passion about the message and care deeply about the people to whom you are delivering that message. This comes across loud and clear. Unfortunately, so does a lack of sincerity or caring! Before you communicate with people, think about what you are trying to convey, why it is important to them, and how you can best help them to digest the message.

Say What You Mean

In the highly political world of business, it is often difficult to decipher the intent of people's messages. That's why it is so important to say what you mean and mean what you say. First of all, you should be honest and forthright in your communication. If something stinks, don't say it smells like a rose. Of course, there is a way to deliver difficult messages in a constructive and professional manner. Clearly, you should use tact. However, you can't leave the conversation thinking one thing and having the person you spoke with think something else.

I had an experience where a client of mine complained to me that another leader within the organization was not providing him the service he required. He asked my advice as to how to deal with this issue. I told him that I would be happy to observe the dynamic between the two of them and provide some feedback and ideas. The next time these two gentlemen met on a "sticky" subject, it just so happened that I was in the room. The client went to great lengths to be respectful and positive with the service provider—so much so, in fact, that the message of how dissatisfied he was with his support was totally diluted. The service provider left the room feeling no particular sense of urgency, and the client left the meeting feeling an escalated level of frustration. I suggested to the client that in his efforts to be professional and keep the service provider's ego intact, he had not delivered his message. I have also seen people yell and scream like lunatics to the point that the actual substance of their message was drowned out by the sheer volume and emotion of their outburst. It is imperative in communicating that you take full responsibility for clearly stating your position and ensuring that the recipient of your message understands and "gets it." I have heard people say that communication is a 50–50 shared responsibility. I disagree! If I am trying to convey a message to someone, the onus is 100 percent on me to accomplish this objective.

Mean What You Say

The second part of my approach is to mean what you say. Later on, we will focus on integrity. People need to know that you are a person of your word and that they can count on what you say being the truth. Therefore, it is absolutely critical to mean what you say. If you intend to accomplish an objective by the end of the month, don't tell people you'll have it done by the end of the week. If someone really screwed up and you are peeved, don't say that it was no big deal and that you are fine with it. Speak the truth. This is a particularly challenging thing to do when you find yourself up against it. The temptation to tell people what they want to hear is overwhelming. I often tell people that my responsibility is to tell them what they need to hear so that they can make informed decisions, as opposed to telling them what they want to hear so that they are misguided to think that everything is going along swimmingly until the train goes off the tracks. It is imperative for leaders to be honest, constructive, and clear to achieve effective communication.

The Importance of Listening

I am a Type-A New Yorker who, over time, has evolved from being a very shy person to one who has learned to love the sound of my own voice! I am certain that I am not alone. Many of us confuse communication with talking. Although delivering a message is certainly an important part of communication, it is only one part. I would argue that it is the least important part. My mother used to tell me, "Larry, God gave you two ears and one mouth. You should use them in that ratio." My mother was a very wise person! Many people view communication as "talking *at* people." The great communicator talks *with* people. That means that they are intently interested in learning about what makes the other person tick and what their concerns may be. Many times, politicians have an agenda that they are attempting to push. Many prospective candidates have seen their campaign crash and burn because their message was not congruent with the concerns of their constituents.

Are you a good listener? Do you give the people you communicate with the space, time, and comfort to share their thoughts? Do you look them in the eye and listen intently when they speak? Do you attempt to process and give feedback regarding what you think they have conveyed? Are you present when you speak with them, or are you multitasking? Do you give them your undivided attention, or are you thinking about the next thing on your to do list? Are you simply waiting for them to stop speaking so that you can start?

This is an area of great challenge for me and one I continue to work on. Being Type A, I always have an agenda I am trying to accomplish. I also speak very fast and don't leave a lot of "dead air" in my conversations. I have observed over time that if I don't make a conscious effort to stop and provide others the opportunity to share their thoughts, my dialogues can quickly turn into monologues! I have also observed that when people sense that you genuinely care about what they think and have to share, they are not only more open to sharing their thoughts with you but they are also more receptive to what you have to share with them. I am reminded (often) by my wife that listening is an active, not a passive, endeavor. She occasionally will tell me, "You aren't listening to me." Being the wiseacre that I am, I will proceed to repeat back to her (almost verbatim) everything she's said to me over the past five minutes. She will then say to me in an exasperated tone, "I know you *heard* me, but you weren't *listening* to me!" We live in a fast-paced, interrupt-driven, noisy world. It's not always easy to take the time to quietly listen to others but it is critical that we do. I have also noticed that many times we have more patience and listen more closely to strangers than we do to the people closest to us, either in our personal or professional lives. Isn't it strange that we will sometimes be more generous with our time and patience with complete strangers than with the people who mean the most to us and have the greatest impact on our success and well-being?

Who Do I Need to Communicate With?

I have seen many so-called leaders only make the time and effort to communicate with those who they feel can do something for them. Let me share a story with you. I once worked with an executive we'll call Ed. Ed was a bright man. However, Ed was only interested in Ed. Ed was interested in forwarding his own agenda. The amount of time, consideration, and kindness he would show a person was based solely by the number of "stripes" the person had on the shoulder of his uniform. One day, Ed saw me speaking with Jim, the person who delivered our interoffice mail. Jim was a very pleasant gentleman who had a developmental disability. In spite of this challenge, he held a job, was gracious to people, and was a positive contributor to society. He and I developed a relationship over time, and I found that he always brightened my day when he came to visit and deliver the mail. After one of my encounters with him, Ed came to talk to me. He shared with me that he couldn't understand why I would "waste my time" talking to this person who obviously couldn't help me in any way. I was flabbergasted by this comment! At the risk of coming across as holier than thou, I believe that all of us add value and are important. Since I genuinely believe this, hopefully it comes across to the people I interact with. Unfortunately for Ed, so do his feelings! If you buy into my premise that leadership is about influence and positively impacting other people's lives, then who do you think has a bigger effect on people's lives—Ed, the guy with an Ivy league education and a position of status, or Jim, a person perhaps with less God-given gifts but more of a sense for what it means to be a human being?

A great leader communicates effectively with everyone around them. They engage their clients, their people, their peers, their management, and others. They take every possible opportunity to make sure that the entire cast of characters in their world feel listened to, understood, and up to speed. A leader doesn't "dole out pearls of wisdom" to the select few on an as-needed basis. She develops relationships with everyone within her sphere of influence.

How Should I Communicate with Them?

Once individuals buy into the need to communicate with others, they often have a question as to the best approach to communicating. This is really two questions in one! The first question is whether to communicate with people on a one-to-one basis or as part of a larger group. The second question is about the best vehicle for communication—conversation, presentation, or the written word. Let's reflect on both of these questions.

Individual versus Group Communication

The decision regarding whether to communicate on an individual basis versus en masse has several variables. There are clearly times when speaking to someone face to face on a one-on-one basis is the right answer. Other times, it is more effective to deliver a message to a larger group. Here are some questions that will help you kickstart your thinking to help determine which approach is best:

- Am I hoping to engage the person in dialogue or simply deliver a monologue?
- How well do I know the person?
- What level of relationship do I have with the individual?
- Is there an existing level of trust?
- Will the group dynamic stimulate interaction and feedback, or will it stifle interaction?
- If I am hoping for feedback, will the key individuals feel more comfortable providing it in private or will they have more comfort sharing their thoughts in a group setting?
- How many people do I need to speak with, in what period of time, and where are they located?

In general, I have found that if you are hoping to engage in meaningful dialogue, don't have a strong existing relationship with the individuals, or are delivering a difficult message, it is often best to have the conversations on a one-to-one basis in a private setting. If instead you are simply sharing an update with a large group of people with whom you have a long track record, a group update might work well.

57

Should I Communicate Via Conversation, Presentation, or the Written Word?

I once worked with an attorney whose response to many of my inquiries was, "It depends." She comes to mind as I attempt to answer this question. Primarily the vehicle for communication should be driven by the nature of the message and the audience. Sending written communiqués is best when providing a large group of people simple information to keep them up to speed. A perfect example of this is sending out a monthly newsletter or updating people regarding project status, service updates, and comings and goings.

Presentations are often most effective when educating or explaining new concepts. For example, if you are trying to explain the benefits of a new project to a board of directors, you may want to incorporate a presentation into your repertoire (of course, only after you have presold the idea to people on an individual basis!). The best way to really reach out to people on a personal level is via conversation. This is clearly the most personal way to connect with an individual, and it allows you to engage them on a much deeper level than the other potential approaches.

How Often Should I Communicate?

Many times, people are reluctant to engage in communication because they feel their message has already been delivered and they fear being redundant. I read somewhere that you have to say something at least seven times before a person internalizes your message. While I don't know what the exact number is, I do know this—you can never overcommunicate (of course, my family may not agree with this statement!). What may seem obvious to you might not be to the other person. Many times, we are too close to the issue to be objective enough to determine how effectively people have digested an idea. You must constantly reinforce your message if you hope other people will begin to internalize it.

Recall from Chapter 3 that perception is reality. I have tried to instill this concept in my team to help them understand how a person's perception of "the facts" is far more important than the actual facts themselves! I once started to have a conversation with a member of my team about a situation when, halfway through my thought, she exclaimed, "I know, I know—perception is reality!" You might think I would be annoyed by this reaction. Truth be told, I was ecstatic! I had clearly gotten this message through to this individual to the point where it was top of mind when dealing with certain situations. I use a litmus test with people to determine how effectively they think their messages have registered with their audience. I'll ask them, "If you woke this person out of a dead sleep at 2 A.M. in the morning and asked them to react to a question, would they be able to respond effectively without pause?" If the answer is not a resounding yes, then you still have work to do! Modifying any behavior, whether it's changing your eating habits (a personal challenge for me!) or learning multiplication tables (an exercise today's youth don't understand!), takes practice and repetition. The key to learning any new behavior is developing new, good habits. Constant reinforcement of your message helps create such habits and learned responses. You will often see a football team be more effective running a two-minute drill at the end of a game than it was for the rest of the game. The reason is that the players constantly practice running this drill because they realize that there is often little time to stop and think under this circumstance. It also helps because they are simply reacting to the situation without overthinking! I am not suggesting that thinking is a bad thing (I try to engage in it occasionally myself!). I am only suggesting that you want to communicate often enough to create immediate, natural reactions and responses to some basic situations. We often practice disaster recovery exercises. Many of us remember this approach in the simple exercise of fire drills that thankfully broke up the school day! The rationale behind this is that the time to figure out how to respond to a crisis is not while the crisis is happening! Repetition is the key (have I said that enough times yet?).

The Need for Marketing

As a Chief Information Officer (CIO), I often have the opportunity to present to fellow technology leaders. Many of these people got into the field of information technology because they were stronger left-brain people and were less comfortable with small talk and banter. On several occasions I have been asked to present on the topic of "Marketing the Value of IT." Whenever I start to speak about marketing, many of the people in the audience either softly groan or roll their eyes. First of all, many of them don't feel they should have to market anything. People should simply understand the importance of their work. Second, most of them got into IT so that they wouldn't have to engage in things like marketing! If they had wanted to be involved in marketing, they would have gotten into . . . well . . . marketing! In order to break down this natural resistance to my message, I often play a little game with them. I will ask the audience, "How many of you are experienced in marketing?" Maybe two or three hands go up in a room of a hundred people. Then I follow up with another question, "How many of you are in a long-term committed relationship?" This time, most of the room raises their hands. I follow up by saying, "So let me ask you the first question one more time: 'How many of you are experienced in marketing?'" I go on to explain that I was fortunate enough to marry a beautiful, intelligent, and lovely woman. If you think that convincing her to marry me did not require marketing, you have another thing coming! Inevitably, I get a chuckle from most of the audience and a lot more hands go up! My point, while it may seem trite, is that all of us at some time or another have engaged in marketing. To me, marketing is articulating a value proposition. It is educating people on why they want to listen to you, buy what you are selling, or sign up for your program. No one can succeed in any endeavor alone. Even a great artist who may toil in solitude needs someone to sell and buy her paintings. We all need the support and goodwill of many people in order to succeed. Marketing is a tool for soliciting that goodwill and support. However, there is a key twist on this theme. Effective marketing is not about why you want people to support you. Instead, it answers the question in their mind, "What's in it for me?" The best marketers don't have to sell their ideas, programs, products, or services. People simply want to buy them!

Marketing serves a number of purposes. First of all, it educates people on the value of the work performed by your team. It helps them understand how what you do either directly or indirectly impacts the bottom line of the organization and its ability to accomplish its mission. Second, it creates the ability to ensure that your people are recognized for their efforts and contributions and allows you to build the platform for ensuring that they are rewarded for their excellence.

Marketing is especially important for IT organizations. Let me share a personal story. I am a ***huge*** hockey fan. I live and die with the New Jersey Devils and watch every minute of playoff hockey I can. During the 2003 Stanley Cup Finals, I was watching my Devils play the Anaheim Ducks (they were the Mighty Ducks at the time) in game six when all of a sudden the picture and audio went dead! I was beside myself (kind of a scary picture there being two of me!). I checked the other TVs in my house and quickly realized that we had lost cable service. I immediately called the cable company. After 20 minutes on hold, I was met on the phone by a less-than-motivated representative who started to explain to me in his vernacular what was wrong. As politely and patiently as I could, I shared with him that I didn't really care what was wrong. I simply wanted to watch the hockey game! Those of us who provide good customer service know what it feels like, and we like to receive it when we are the customer.

For many executives, IT is viewed as a utility. How do you think about utilities? When do you think about utilities? The only time most people think about the cable company is like me, when they lose service! If the only data point your clients, executives, and board has regarding IT is when something goes wrong, how do you think they view you? Marketing the 99 percent of what goes right in a non-self-serving way helps them have a fuller and more accurate perspective on the value of IT.

Let me share an example of effective marketing. As CIO of the USTA, my team is accountable for providing the technology to help run the most highly attended annual sporting event in the world. One year, we worked with our major clients to develop a video outlining some of the things we have done to help them run the tournament. The stars of this video were some of our key business partners. Their testimonials were unscripted. Their messages were powerful. They shared some of the capabilities we had partnered with and how these services and systems impacted revenue, cut costs, facilitated operations, and overall allowed them to run an effective event. Our business partners were the stars of the video because they deserved a great deal of the credit for the success. They were also very credible voices to our community. Having them share their thoughts on the value of our joint efforts and the investments we had partnered on to innovate and improve our event provided a powerful message to our leadership.

Through the Lens of the CIO – How Comfortable Are You with Blowing Your Own Horn?

Most of us were raised to believe that hard work was the key to success and that if we simply did a good job, we would be recognized and rewarded for it. We were also taught that self-promotion was at best gauche and at worst unprofessional. I remember very early on learning the acronym SPS: self-praise stinks! Because of these early lessons, it is often very difficult for CIOs to comfortably and effectively market the successes of their team and the value that they bring to their organizations. Add to this a basic level of shyness or discomfort many CIOs have in publicly delivering "pitches" and you see we may have a challenge on our hands. I would suggest looking at this through a different prism.

First of all, to me, marketing is not self-promotion but education. An effective marketer focuses on articulating a value proposition. She is not concerned with getting pats on the back or on hearing how wonderful she is. She is simply educating an audience. Her focus is not on herself but on delivering a message of value to her audience. Remember, first and foremost, we are business leaders. As such, we have a responsibility to ensure that our leadership and board of directors understand the value that is being created based on the investments they make. For each business project that relies on technology, it is our responsibility to articulate, in business terms, what the required investment is, what we have done with this money, and what benefits the organization has gleaned from this investment. If you met with your financial planner, you would want to know what he did with your money and how it has helped you get closer to accomplishing your financial objectives. How is this any different?

Another reason you need to be comfortable marketing the progress you make is that you are responsible for the professional development and success of your team. These people trust you to represent them in such a way that the organization understands the value they bring so that they can be recognized, rewarded and compensated appropriately for their contributions. Try getting a promotion for technologists when nobody knows who they are or understands what they do. As a leader, you owe it to your people to represent them effectively so that they can grow and reap the appropriate rewards of their efforts.

(continued)

(*Continued*)

Finally, if these two arguments don't persuade you to be willing to market your efforts, let me leave you with this thought. Every day, large outsource companies such as IBM and Hewlett-Packard are whispering into the ears of your board members about how wonderful life would be if they ran your technology services. Now don't get me wrong, I am a big believer in appropriately leveraging outsource partners to drive value. But if all your leadership ever hears from you is the problems you are challenged with, and all they ever hear from vendors is how rosy life would be if they simply turned the keys over to them, what conclusions do you think your leadership will eventually reach? If you are reluctant to market the value your team delivers, just remember that there are highly compensated and skilled marketing professionals with big budgets from large technology companies who are happy to take this problem off your hand!

What Is Your Brand?

These days, there is much more of a focus on what I will refer to as *personal branding*. We all know about product branding. Some companies go to great lengths to convey a message that their brand is about reliability. Others focus on the cache associated with their product being hip or cool. Whatever the case, companies spend a lot of effort and even more money to develop and articulate a brand strategy.

It is equally important to develop and communicate a personal brand. I suggest to my clients that they ask themselves a few questions:

- What do I want people to think when they see me?
- What are the words I want people to use to describe their experience with me?
- Who am I, and what am I all about?

I often go through an exercise with my clients where I ask them to come up with three words they want people to associate with them. For me, these three words are:

1. *Integrity*—I want people to feel that they are always working with a person of character who is dependable and honest.
2. *Passion*—I am a high-energy, passionate person. I want people to know that I will attack whatever objective they entrust to me with a great deal of passion and focus.
3. *Results*—It is important to me that the people in my life know that they can count on me to consistently deliver results. No excuses, no BS . . . I will deliver for them.

What are your three words? What do people think of you today? Is there a gap between people's current perception of you and how you want them to think of you? What are you doing about it? Branding is an essential function for every executive. You need to spend some time and energy creating your brand and working to become your brand.

Leading a Volunteer Army

Many of us who are baby boomers grew up at a time when the prevailing approach to managing people was command and control. Management told us what to do, how to do it, and when to do it. We did as we were told and were rewarded with a paycheck every two weeks. Those of us who interact with millennials know that this approach doesn't play well with this new generation of workers! One of the many wonderful things about living in America is that we have options. Therefore, the people who we lead also have options. One of their options is to jump ship if they feel they are working for someone who doesn't value, appreciate, or understand them. I always try to remember that the people who I am fortunate enough to lead are a volunteer army. Therefore, my approach as a leader is not to co-erce them to do my bidding but, rather, to motivate them to do what is not just in the organization's best interest but, more im-portantly, in *their* best interest!

I would strongly suggest that this approach is not only effec-tive in dealing with our colleagues but also with dealing with our significant others and children. I once heard a story about a very accomplished and educated man who was trying to get his horse to go back to the stable. No matter how much he pulled and prodded, the horse would not budge! A young farmhand saw his dilemma and she simply held a carrot in front of the horse and gently led it back into the stable. As a leader, how much carrot are we using versus how much stick? As Dale Carnegie once wrote, "You attract more flies with honey than with vinegar."

Through the Lens of the CIO—Are Your People Spreading the Gospel?

A number of years ago, I was part of a task force that was re-sponsible for making a decision on which browser should be used by our clients. This was long before the Internet was a per-vasive force and every device from a laptop to a blender came with a browser imbedded in it. The task force was sponsored by our VP of IT, who acted as our de-facto CIO. One of the mem-bers of the task force was a gentleman who was the most bril-liant technologist I have ever met. He understood the potential impact of the Internet at a time when most of us thought the ini-tials *www* stood for a wrestling organization! Brilliant as he was, he had one fatal flaw—he was not a team player. The task force decided to leverage a particular browser technology not neces-sarily because it was the best technical solution but because there was economic value in the decision as well as a support infrastructure in the industry that would allow us to better serve our clients. The decision was made, and the task force meeting adjourned. As we walked to the elevators, someone approached my brilliant technologist friend and asked him what he should do about getting a browser. The gentleman told him to purchase a totally different solution than the standard the task force had decided to deploy!

Why am I sharing this long story? The bottom line is that regardless of how compelling a CIO's homilies are to his community, what really matters to your audience is what your people are saying day in and day out in the quiet conversations that happen in hallways and cafeterias. You can be the most motivational evangelist in the world and blow people away from the pulpit, but the greatest impact happens when people talk one on one.

Are your people on board with your program? Do they buy into what you are selling? What do they say to your clients when you are not in the room? I had a wonderful experience a few years back. I overheard a conversation between one of my technical leads and one of our senior clients. They were discussing a particular strategy that we were planning to implement. My staff member shared our vision nearly verbatim as to how I had explained it to my team. I knew at that point that he had bought into "the program" and that I could count on him to help us lead the type of change we were hoping to implement.

It's not enough for you to be an effective evangelist as CIO. You must work to create evangelists throughout your organization who will help you spread your gospel of transformational change. No one can drive positive change alone; it takes a team. Is your team on board? Do they represent your vision? What do they say in the quiet moments when you can't hear them?

Communicating Tough Messages

It would be wonderful if all of our communications were positive. We would all like to live in a place where all projects were successes, everyone did a great job all of the time, obstacles simply melted away, and the streets were paved with gold. Anyone over the age of three knows that this place simply does not exist. Life is challenging. Good people make bad choices. Things don't always go as planned (as a matter of fact they rarely do!). There will be many times as a leader that you will either have to communicate difficult messages because of the circumstances or because you need to deliver a personal message to an individual that he or she may not want to hear. While this is never fun, the way you handle these opportunities is often the difference between building credibility and long-term success versus resentment and mistrust.

The first suggestion I would share is to never take the "ostrich approach" to leadership. Too often, I have seen leaders try to bury their heads in the sand in the hope that the challenging situation or behavior will simply blow over. Their thought process suggests, "Maybe if I ignore it, it will go away!" My experience is that problems are like a curable cancer. If ignored, they will not only fester but will worsen until they consume the entire organism. However, if treated early and aggressively, they can be eliminated and the person or team can go on to live a long, successful life. Therefore, when you are confronted with a challenging dynamic, the best approach, in my opinion, is to proactively work to nip it in the bud.

The way you go about communicating in these situations will say a great deal about the type of leader and, more importantly, the type of person you are. Let's take two types of examples and reflect on how to best handle them.

First, let's focus on having to share bad news. As I am writing this book, we are all living through perhaps the greatest economic issues since the Great Depression. This has caused many organizations to have to rationalize their costs and make budget and headcount reductions. I have had to do exactly the same thing. The first thing you need to do in this situation is to honestly communicate the situation. What is happening? Why? What has led to this scenario? What steps are you planning to take? How does this impact the people on your team? How long do we expect this situation to last? For those who are being directly impacted, why were these choices made? For those indirectly impacted, what lies ahead for them? Is this the first phase of a wave of reductions? Am I safe? Will I be able to succeed in this environment? Will I be next? Should I be looking for a new opportunity? All of these are legitimate questions that will be running through the minds of your people. You need to get in front of things and answer these questions before they get asked. You need to let people know what to expect. You need to calm the storm and keep people's focus on the task at hand. Most importantly, you need to elicit their support to make them partners in fixing the problem, as opposed to victims of circumstance. Ignoring the issue or glossing it over will simply magnify their concerns and have them heading for the exits! You can either get in front and lead the parade or expect to get trampled by the elephants! Publicly sharing your thoughts in a group setting and also reassuring people on an individual basis is the tact to be taken in these situations.

The second example is a more personal one. Very few people, me included, enjoy confrontations. We rather not have to deal with people one on one to share bad news. However, as a leader you sometimes have to share difficult messages. What do you do if a person is underperforming and not accomplishing their objectives? Once again, ignoring the situation is not the answer. Not only does their lack of performance impact you, but it also impacts the rest of the team who are working hard to accomplish the mission. Ignoring the situation is unfair to the majority of people who are pulling their weight and making things happen. A leader takes a person aside in a private and dispassionate way to share concerns and expectations. They give others an opportunity to share their side of the story. Perhaps some mitigating circumstances are at play that should be addressed. Perhaps the individual doesn't even realize there is a problem. Perhaps they don't care! Whatever the situation, you need to clearly and directly articulate your concern, the impact of the behavior, and your expectations of what must be done to improve the situation and within what timeframes.

Focusing on the Issue, Not the Person

I learned the hard way by screwing up many times how easily you can damage a relationship. The easiest way to hurt someone's feelings and your goodwill is to focus on and attack them as people. All of us like to think that we are nice, good, hardworking people. When we feel under attack, we lash out and retaliate. However, most of us are objective enough to realize that even when we try our best, we sometimes miss the mark. Focusing not on the individual but on the issue has helped me develop better relationships and more successful outcomes.

I have also noticed an insidious dynamic. Many times we are more patient and positive with total strangers or people we interact with at work than with the members of our own families and the people we love the most. We seem to use up all of our patience and skills at work and then come home and act horribly with our loved ones. No matter how close you are to someone, you still need to be caring about how you deliver your messages. Always focus on the issue and never on the person. Let's see if you can feel the difference between these statements:

"You are inconsiderate!" versus "I would appreciate it if you would please put the seat down!"

"You don't care about me!" versus "It hurts my feelings when you speak ill of my family."

"That's the dumbest idea I've ever heard!" versus "Perhaps there is a different approach we can take."

"You are lazy!" versus "I think we need to work on that issue a little harder."

"You always take the easy way out," versus "There may be a
better way to address the issue for the long term."

"You're a failure!" versus "This wasn't your best effort but
I'm sure you'll improve next time."

Honesty and Transparency

Many leaders are guilty of the next sin even though they are well
intentioned. Instead of honestly sharing their concerns, they try to
sugarcoat the situation. Things aren't really that bad. They are
bound to get better. It's only a temporary blip. This is one of the
most delicate balancing acts a leader will ever have to navigate. On
the one hand, a leader needs to be optimistic, keep the team calm,
and articulate the expectation that things will turn around and the
team will succeed. On the other hand, a leader also must be honest.
Lying about your own concerns is dishonest, and people can see
right through you. However, panicking and yelling "fire" is not the
answer, either! Let me share an example from my own experience.

When I took my current job I walked into what I can only
describe as the most dysfunctional organization I had ever seen.
Nothing was working. Our clients thought we were idiots. Client
satisfaction was terrible. Projects routinely came in late, over
budget, and under value. The team had no credibility. My office
had no relationships with the leadership of the organization. All
in all, it was quite a mess! For me to tell everyone that things
were fine and that everything was great would have been a lie
and stupidity on my part. However, running out of the building
screaming wasn't going to help matters! I simply made it a point
to build a reputation of being someone who was honest, constructive, and transparent. Where there were problems, I admit-
ted we had an issue but quickly refocused people as to our plans
to address the issue. When we made progress, we communicated it. When we screwed up, we honestly stated our mistake,
shared why the issue occurred, and listed the steps we were

taking to ensure there would not be a recurrence. We instituted Client Satisfaction Scorecards, which we administered twice a year. This allowed our clients to share their thoughts, frustrations, and suggestions with us. We then would publicly report not only the results of the scorecard but also every single comment we received! Many of my peers thought I was crazy! Why would you hang out your dirty laundry for all to see?

I was trying to develop a reputation for honesty and transparency. If people knew they could trust me to speak the truth when things were bad, they would also trust me to share honest results of our progress. It's also harder to take shots at a person who is being open than someone who is trying to hide from the heat. Over time, this approach built our team a great deal of goodwill and credibility in the organization. I became known as a person who was honest and trustworthy. Many people embraced us and supported our team as we worked through the issues and evolved into a high-performance team.

I will summarize this thought by reminding you of a catch phrase I use all the time: "Say what you mean, and mean what you say." Most people have a built-in BS-ometer! They can tell when you are blowing smoke up their clothes, and they resent it. Leaders with integrity communicate honestly, transparently, and constructively.

Lessons Learned

- No matter how good a job you do, you will be measured by how effectively you can communicate your progress and your results. Moreover, your message will only be as effective as the level of integrity you are perceived as having with your audience.
- God gave you two ears and one mouth! The most important aspect of communication is carefully listening to

what your key stakeholders need and expect from you. People will tell you everything you need to know to succeed if you just listen!

- As CIO, you should speak with people at every level in an organization. This also includes your ultimate customers/consumers who reside outside of the organization.

- You need to tailor the delivery of your message to your targeted audience. Different people learn different ways, and you should adapt your message to ensure that it resonates with those you are trying to influence.

- It is critical to communicate often and to ensure that you are constantly on theme and deliver a consistent set of messages.

- As CIO, you need to learn how to effectively market the work your team is performing and the impact that effort has on the bottom line of your organization.

- All executives have a personal brand. Do you know what your brand is with your leadership? What are you doing to enhance your brand?

- The people who work for us do so out of choice. We need to treat them as volunteers and make sure that they are always excited about re-upping for another tour of duty!

- When communicating difficult messages, you should focus on the issue and not on the person. Problems don't get better with time! You should deal with them quickly, constructively, and honestly.

- Honesty and transparency are the hallmark of the way a true leader communicates. Never BS people. Say what you mean, and mean what you say.

CHAPTER 5

Relationship Management

The longer I work in corporate America, the more I have come to realize that business is not conducted between companies but between people. In this chapter, we will cover the topics of building and managing relationships. Specifically, we will focus on the following concepts:

- ❏ Discussing why a leader cannot achieve success alone
- ❏ Focusing your energies on helping other people succeed
- ❏ Being a team builder
- ❏ Building credibility
- ❏ Exploring the focus of every human being: What's in it for me?
- ❏ Serving as a form of leadership
- ❏ Exploring the expression, "It's not about you"
- ❏ Reviewing perception versus reality: Why what people feel about you matters so much

Building successful win–win relationships is not just satisfying but is one of the key components of success for any leader. In spite of this, it never ceases to amaze me how many people undervalue the importance of building genuine positive relationships. I'm not talking about the shaking hands and icebreaker exercises that are prevalent at many conferences and large corporate meetings. My focus is on taking the time and effort to get to know what matters to people and working to help them meet their objectives. If you truly hope to be an effective leader, you need to invest time and effort into building lasting relationships.

No Man (or Woman) Is an Island

The American credo places a high emphasis on being independent and forging one's own way in the world. We are regaled with stories of our forefathers who were pioneers who set out with a small wagon train and settled the West. Although this style of American tale is romantic and energizing, it is not the stuff that modern-day successes are made of! I have had the pleasure to work in the sports and entertainment industry for the past nine years. Our sport, tennis, can be viewed as one of the most individual of all sports. After all, the combatants stand before the crowds alone, seemingly with nothing to support them but a tightly strung racquet! However, if you look a little closer, even in this most individual of sports, success requires the support of a team. World-class tennis players usually have a team composed of trainers, nutritionists, coaches, racquet stringers, and other subject matter experts. A player's popularity also depends to a large degree on his or her relationship with the media and the fans. Even the most gifted champion will have limited opportunities off the court in terms of endorsements or sponsorships if he or she isn't considered fan friendly. Before tennis players ever set foot on the blue courts of the U.S. Open, they have worked with countless coaches, probably in numerous tennis academies over the course of their youth. They have had special teaching or tutoring to help them navigate their educational requirements and have needed the financial and moral support of their families to get to this point. As you can see, even in what many would consider one of the most individual of sports, success requires a team. One of my constant messages to my team is that success is a team sport. Let's focus a little on the aspects that make up successful relationship management.

Helping Other People Succeed

One can argue that human nature is somewhat selfish. No matter how altruistic you are, at the end of the day most people are primarily concerned with how things in life impact them. We all view life through our own eyes and see the world unfolding through the backdrop of our own screenplay. Every day we wake up focused on our goals, our needs, our challenges, and our relationships. Here's a little secret—so does everyone else!

Early in my life I had an experience that taught me an important lesson about success. In my early teenage years I played some organized hockey. This was before five dislocated shoulders and two broken ankles derailed my dream of playing in the NHL! One year, I was named captain of my team. I worked my tail off to improve my skills. I hit the weight room to be strong enough to play in front of the net. All of this effort paid off in my leading the league in scoring that year. Unfortunately, my team was mediocre and we missed the playoffs that year. This was a tremendous disappointment to me, but I took some solace in the fact that as the leagues' leading scorer, I was certain to win the MVP award. I sat next to my coach at the awards banquet thinking about what I would say and who I would thank when my name was called for the MVP award. When that moment came, the master of ceremonies introduced another player! How could that be? I led the league in scoring! I had ten more goals than my closest competitor! What the heck? I turned to my coach utterly dumbfounded and asked him how this could be happening. He shared with me words that have lasted a lifetime: "Larry, there are no winners on a losing team."

Success is indeed a team sport. If you hope to experience a modicum of personal success, your focus must be on other people. When I started my current position, there was a great deal of negative energy between the business executives we supported and the IT group. There was a great deal of finger pointing, and we engaged in what we lovingly call *the blame game.* There were plenty of reasons (or excuses) on both sides why IT had failed to live up to the needs and expectations of the organization. One of the first things I tried to do was to stop my people from engaging in this dynamic and have them simply focus on helping our clients meet their objectives. I worked to develop relationships with people throughout the organization to see what their goals were and how we could support them. We started by solving simple problems and building the credibility required to allow them to entrust larger issues to us. When a project succeeded, I made sure that our business partners received the appropriate recognition for the success. I also made sure that my own team received the kudos they deserved for their role in the effort. I never focused on my own success. My thought process is that if you help other people succeed, your own success takes care of itself.

This concept of taking your eyes off yourself and focusing on someone else works in every aspect of life. Many of us are in long-term, committed relationships. Few people in committed relationships are getting the level of satisfaction they would like from their relationships. Most of them are focused on what their significant other isn't doing for them to make them happy. Well, guess what: If both people are focused this way, then no one is happy! I am not suggesting that we should all turn into Mother Teresa and be totally selfless and only focus on the needs of others. I am simply stating that if we focus on supporting the needs of others, somehow our own needs are more likely to find a way of getting met. Some people refer to this as karma. I am not spiritually mature enough to know what it is—but I know that it's true! If you are unhappy with the dynamic in your relationships, spend some time focusing on making the other person happy and see what happens.

Being a Team Builder

As we have already discussed, in all aspects of life success is built on the efforts of a team. One of the best reputations you can develop as a leader is someone who is a *team builder*. Team builders care about their colleagues' success. Team builders look for ways to help others grow and develop. They make sure that other people are recognized for their contributions. They talk others up and always have a constructive word that buoys people's spirits. Now trust me, those who know me will tell you that I am far from a Pollyanna personality! I am as grumpy and moody as the next guy! But my interactions with people are constructive and are focused on positive outcomes. Granted, there will always be a handful of people who, no matter how you act, will be jackasses (sorry . . . I couldn't think of a more politically correct term!). My experience suggests that this group is in the minority. Most people react positively to team players and team builders. They appreciate the support and recognition you provide and look forward to opportunities to work with you.

One of the most rewarding experiences I had was at a time when I worked in the pharmaceutical industry. As part of the corporate IT function, we were held in low regard by the business unit leaders. In particular, we were viewed very negatively by the human pharmaceutical group. I worked hard to build a team dynamic with these people, in spite of the legacy culture and track record. We engaged in a very challenging project with the head of the Asia/Pacific IT group. He was a bright but tough "no-nonsense" individual. I made sure that my team worked to build a team dynamic with him and his people. The project had its challenges, but we met them head on instead of pointing fingers. At the end of the project, this gentleman gave me one of the best compliments I have ever received in the workplace: "Larry, not only did your team do a great job, but you guys were a pleasure to work with. I look forward to working together on our next project." I am delighted to say that this person became a friend, and more than a decade later, we still get together and enjoy each other's company.

There is an old expression that a rising tide lifts all ships. When you focus on ensuring that the team wins and that they get the recognition they deserve, good things will happen for you as well. One of the great traditions in all of sports is how the hockey team that wins the NHL championship is recognized with the Stanley Cup. First of all, every member of the winning team gets to carry the cup as he skates around the hockey rink. Then the entire team, from the equipment managers to the superstar goalie to the coaches, gets to take a team picture with the Stanley Cup. Finally, every player from the winning team has his name etched on the Stanley Cup so that people can see it for the rest of time. It is amazing how emotional and personal an experience this is for the players.

I remember the first time the New Jersey Devils won the Stanley Cup in 1995. There was a player on the Devils named Mike Peluso. Mike wasn't the prettiest skater on the team or the most skilled offensive player. His role was as the enforcer on the team. He was tough as nails and was responsible for "taking out the dirty laundry" when opposing players got too physical with his teammates. It was not uncommon to see Mike exchanging "pleasantries" by dropping his gloves and punching out an opposing player. Mike was not the kind of person you would want to annoy in a crowded bar. As tough as he was, it was incredible to watch him break down like a baby and cry his eyes out when he lifted the Stanley Cup. He was clearly overcome with emotion; this was a life-changing experience for him.

Just think how infrequently people are recognized in life. Most times, if you do what you're supposed to do you get taken for granted. It is rare that people get to spend a moment in the sun. As a leader, it is imperative that you celebrate your team's victories. Make sure that the team receives the credit and recognition they deserve. Make sure everyone knows the impact of the work the team completed. And most importantly, make sure that the members of the team feel appreciated and valued for the contributions they made to the team's success.

Being a team builder means that you share the credit for success. It means you recognize people's contributions to the process. It means your focus is on the team and not on yourself or your selfish motivations. Ask yourself a question: What kind of team would you like to play on? What kind of leader would you like to work for? What kind of dynamic would you like to be a part of? Being a team builder means being the change you want to see in others. OK—I'll get off my soapbox now!

Building Credibility

There's an old expression that what you do speaks so loud I can't hear what you say! Don't get me wrong, effective communication and inspiring people is certainly an important part of effective leadership. However, all the motivational speeches in the world can't make up for a lack of credibility.

There are no shortcuts to building credibility. It is a process that evolves a day at a time. Credibility speaks to trust. When you are credible, people know they can trust your words because experience suggests that you back them up with actions that are congruent with your words. One of the best steps you can take to building credibility is building transparence. Let me share an example.

When I began in my current position I was told that the people who had resided in my office (and there had been three in five years!) had no relationship with our board or our business leaders. They didn't communicate very often, and on the rare occasion they did, they spoke in geek speak, a language that is not about business but about acronyms! One of the first things I attempted to do was to build an ongoing communication process with total transparency. As I mentioned in Chapter 4, we published not only the quantitative results of our scorecards but also every single comment we received from our clients (and believe me, we received some beauties!). I was trying to build credibility with my audience. I knew that if I was brutally honest about the feedback we were receiving and what was wrong with the current state, that these people would reward us with trust.

When you work with people you trust, you are more open to what they have to share. You are also more willing to work with them because you don't have to question if they have another agenda! When things went wrong (and believe me, they did!), I would communicate what had happened, why it happened, and what we planned to do to ensure there wasn't a reoccurrence of the issue. People started to understand that they could take my words to the bank. Another positive benefit of building credibility is that it provides you a platform to lobby from. When we started making real progress in turning things around, I wanted to ensure that the people on my team responsible for this transformation were recognized and rewarded. Having credibility provided me the platform as well as the goodwill to make this happen.

Credibility is something that is hard to win but easy to lose. One slip-up where you act in a way that is not consistent with the persona you are trying to project can set you back to square one. That is why it is so vital to be honest and consistent in your dealings. Besides, at my age it's impossible to keep track of too many lies! Kidding aside, people need to know what's in your heart. I've heard many people say that it's a mistake to be too open and get too close to people in a professional setting. You need to keep a safe distance and take a clinical approach to working with people. Perhaps that's true if you are an emergency room doctor! However, my experience has told me that the more you care about people and the more they care about you, the easier it is to get things done.

As I've shared with my team many times and discussed in depth in Chapter 4 (I'm sure they are sick of hearing it!), say what you mean and mean what you say. Too many times we must attempt to interpret the true meaning behind people's words. People who I work with have come to realize that what I say is really what I mean and what they can expect me to do. That, in my mind, is the essence of credibility.

The Law of WIFM—What's in it for Me?

Whether people are open enough to say it or not, every one of us in every relationship or interaction is focused on a single question: "What's in it for me?" Whether you are dating someone new, negotiating with your long-term partner, or interviewing for a position, both parties are focused on the value they hope to receive from the potential relationship or interaction. Knowing this is a powerful tool in interpersonal relationships.

What's in it for Them?

When you engage someone, whether it is a new relationship or a new project with an old colleague, the first question you should ask yourself, "What's in it for them?" What does the other person hope to get out of the interaction with you? How can others benefit from working with you? What can you do that will make a tangible difference in their success? We all have a personal agenda. We are all more interested in our own objectives than in other people's. We all want to work with people who are willing and able to help us forward our agendas and accomplish our objectives. As a leader and an effective executive, you need to develop a reputation as one of those people. The problem is, most of us are so focused on what's in it for us that we never achieve those results! It has been my experience that the best way to get what you need is to help others get what they need. This is not meant as a path to sainthood but as a pragmatic approach to being effective in the hard, cold world of business.

Through the Lens of the CIO—How Do Vendors Do It?

We are talking a great deal about the need for and value of relationship management in this chapter. This is not always an easy skill for many CIOs. Perhaps a good way to learn how to be more effective at this skill is to reflect on people who are good at it and do it for a living—the sales professionals that you deal with from your vendor community.

We've all seen and dealt with bad salespeople. They are very easy to spot, and they leave us cold. What makes someone a bad salesperson? Let's think about some of our experiences. Most ineffective salespeople are focused on themselves. It's all about them and what their company sells. They call on you without knowing who you are, what makes you tick, or what your real objectives, challenges, or opportunities are. Their entire focus is on getting in front of you to tell you what they can sell, as opposed to what you may need.

Now let's think about the effective relationship managers you have worked with. First of all, they take the time to get to know you both as a person as well as a professional. They spend time listening to understand what your challenges are and what your focus is to drive value. Over time, once they better understand your needs and opportunities, they will present ways that they may be able to help you solve problems. As they get to know you as an individual, they may turn you on to a soccer camp they found out about where your little Susie may want to enroll. They tell you about an SAT tutor their kid went to who may be able to help your son Frank get his math scores up. They truly take the time and effort to develop a relationship with you so that you will think of them when opportunities and challenges arise.

Let me share an example. I spent ten years working at a major global pharmaceutical firm. During my tenure, I spent a stint running global network services. I had the pleasure to work with a gentleman from Cisco Systems named Tom. Tom was a passionate salesperson who always made me aware of Cisco's products and how they might support me. But more than that, Tom got to know who I was, how I was wired, what mattered to me, and what ways he could add value to me both personally and professionally. When I left this company, Tom still remained in touch and we became friends. Roll the tape forward a few years. I am now the CIO in my current organization. We are experiencing a major network-related issue during our premier event, which will determine the kind of financial year we will have as a company. What did I do? Did I call my new Cisco rep who, other than drop by to make a standard sales call, wouldn't be able to pick me out of a police lineup? No—I called Tom. I told Tom the pickle I was in and asked if he knew a firm who had the engineering and architectural knowhow to help me dig out from under. That night, a team of people from a Cisco VAR arrived on my campus to help us put out the fire and rethink how we architected our solution.

Remember to take the time and effort to get to know your clients as people as well as professionals and to be the person who they know they can count on when the proverbial stuff hits the fan. That is effective relationship management.

But Enough about Me . . . What Do You Think about Me?

This is the first cousin to our last topic. Most people are self-absorbed. It's not that we are bad people, it's just that there is no subject more interesting to us than ourselves! We live in a self-centered universe where people view the happenings of the day through their own lenses and determine how they feel about events based on the impact they have on their own agenda.

In working with people, it is important to spend most of your time and focus on the other person's interests and objectives. There are legions of women who have experienced dates with men who spent the whole time talking about themselves! I'm sure that these men ended the evening feeling they had a great time. I'm not as sure that their dates would agree! If you really want to develop goodwill with people and have them look forward to working with you, focus on them, not yourself. By the way, this is a lot easier to say than it is to do! As my wife reminds me quite often, I am an only child. That means I grew up thinking the world revolved around me. After all . . . who else would it be revolving around? It is especially difficult for someone like me to take this tack. I will also openly admit (I feel like this is confession!) that I am much better at doing this at work than I am at home. One of my challenges is that I have come to truly love the sound of my own voice. I almost always have something to say (again . . . just ask my wife). It is a real challenge for me to make sure that I give the other person in a conversation more runway than I take. This is even more of a challenge with my own people. It's easier for me to be gracious with airtime when I am speaking with my board members or my management than with the people on my team. After all, they work for me right? Wrong! A real leader works for his/her team, not vice versa. This is a critical area of development, and one I must continue to work on.

Leading by Serving

Too many people aspire to leadership positions because of the perceived perks of leadership. They see leadership as a privilege. They expect people to bow to them and treat them with kid gloves and sprinkle special treatment on them. Leadership is not a privilege. It is a responsibility. When you are leading people, you are responsible for their development, their professional growth, their success, and to a real degree, their employment. Your people will take their cues from you. You are responsible for setting an example for them. Ultimately, your job is to develop new leaders from among your people.

Servant Leadership

As a leader your role is to serve the team, not to be served by them. You should be asking your people questions like these:

- How can I help you?
- What obstacle can I help remove?
- What resources/tools do you need from me?
- What is holding you back?
- What relationships can I help broker on your behalf?

I have had the great fortune to work for some fine leaders as well as some terrible leaders. In both cases, I have learned from the experience. Servant leadership is the term used to describe an underlying philosophy of listening, empowering, and setting an example.

Never about You

Perhaps the greatest lesson I have learned was from my first manager out of college. He knew enough to never take himself too seriously as a leader. He shared a pearl of wisdom with me that has served me well for almost 30 years. I will pass it along to you. This gentleman said, *"When you are a leader, it's never about you."*

These are powerful words. They focus on the need for true leaders to take their eyes off of themselves and focus on helping others succeed. It's about making sure your people succeed, your clients succeed, and your shareholders succeed. It's about laying the foundation and clearing the path so that obstacles have been removed and people can focus on driving value. True leaders who live to serve know this secret and live it every day.

What People Feel about You Is More Important than Reality

About six months into my tenure as CIO, I noticed a very interesting dynamic. Our clients and our management felt more positively about the progress we had made to date than was actually warranted. That is not to suggest that we hadn't made progress—we certainly had. The team had worked very hard to create a new client-focused attitude and had started to improve many of our services and processes. The reality is that we had probably moved from being a 4 to being a 7 (using Olympic scoring!). However, many of our clients would rate us an 8 or higher! Why this disconnect?

As we discussed in Chapter 3, perception is reality. Let me say that again so it sinks in: Perception *is* reality. How many times have you seen someone tried in the court of public opinion before they ever have a chance to defend themselves in an actual court of law? What people feel about you outweighs the facts! Now clearly, over time enough facts can change people's perceptions. However, as many have stated in other leadership books, first people buy into the leader, then they buy into the message. Creating goodwill and being someone that people trust and like are critical to providing you the time and space you need to make a difference.

We are emotional creatures. We work more from feelings than from logic. In order to create the runway you need to really have an impact; you need to create the goodwill and relationships that will make people want you to succeed and make them want to help you succeed.

I've already discussed how much IT people love discussing metrics. Have you ever watched an IT executive have a conversation with her executives or board about SLAs? It gives new meaning to the expression *eyes glazing over.* People will either go to sleep on you, look at you like you have two heads, or scratch their heads trying to figure out what you are talking about. The only metrics I talk to my key stakeholders about are those that resonate with them. I talk about revenue created, costs savings, return on investment, opportunity costs, you know—business stuff!

To me, the most important metric for an IT executive is what I lovingly refer to as the *hallway metric.* When my clients see me in the hallway, what do they do? How do they react? Do they quickly turn and run in the other direction hoping I didn't see them so that they can avoid me altogether? Do they approach me with the intention of either strangling me or giving me a piece of their mind because of something they perceived we screwed up? Or do they approach me in a friendly manner, shake my hand, and exchange pleasantries? One of the best ways to gauge your progress and your likability factor is by applying the hallway metric. In my opinion, at the end of the day this is the only metric that really matters!

Through the Lens of the CIO—Relationships Trump Metrics!

Virtually every CIO I know is a big fan of metrics. We measure everything from system uptime to mean time to failure and everything else in between. Metrics (as long as they are the right metrics . . . more to come on that) are important. But I experienced a situation that helped me understand that relationships are more important than metrics. Let me explain.

When I arrived in my current role, I inherited a train wreck! I can honestly say that I had never seen a more dysfunctional IT organization. There were problems everywhere, cost overruns,

(continued)

(Continued)

and no relationships with the core business leader . . . all in all a big mess. In Chapter 4, I discussed how we created and administered an IT scorecard based on the issues that our client community felt were most important. We measured service-related satisfaction, quantitative feedback, as well as qualitative aspects of our services such as communication and responsiveness. The scores we received were in the low 3s on a scale of 1 to 5 where 1 is awful and 5 is outstanding. Honestly, the only reason they were even that high was because I was on my "honeymoon" and people were taking pity on me! We also asked for, and received, a great deal of comments, which we published to our community. Many of these comments were quite colorful and quite awful to read.

Six months went by and we administered a follow-up scorecard exercise. During this time we had developed and articulated a game plan to transform IT from a train wreck to a valued service provider to, over time, a trusted business partner. Although we had started to make progress and address some low-hanging fruit, I can assure you than there was still much work to be done.. However, the scores we received went from the low 3s to around 4! Amazing! I must be a miracle worker! Were things really that much better? Perhaps the key to understanding these results were to be found in the comments:

- "IT finally understands us and takes the time to talk to us about our needs and objectives."
- "I appreciate how well you have started to communicate with us and let us know what we are doing and how it affects us."
- "It is great that there is finally someone at the wheel who gets it."

Of course, a few of them went into chapter and verse on various services like e-mail or network access. Most of them, however, commented on issues related to relationships that we had built with them over these six months. The bottom line was, a lot of the progress we had made in terms of client satisfaction was not because our operational service metrics had improved so much (they had gotten a bit better), but because we had taken the time and effort to build relationships with our key stakeholders. They perceived that we cared about their business and were working hard to earn their trust. So you tell me, what is more important, metrics or relationships?

Lessons Learned

- Leaders need the engagement and support of many different groups of people to accomplish their objectives.
- In order for you to reach your goals, you must first help others reach theirs! Effective leaders take their eyes off themselves and focus on helping others succeed.
- Great leaders are team builders. They make sure that others get the visibility, recognition, and rewards they deserve. They are focused on team success, not on their own agenda.
- In order for others to follow you, you need to build personal credibility with them.
- Every human being is focused on WIFM—What's in it for me? As a leader, your focus needs to be on what's in it for others, not for yourself.
- Leaders focus on serving others, not on being served themselves. When you take care of others, your agenda will get taken care of in the process. When you are a leader, it's **never** about you!
- How people feel about you can be more important than the hard facts. People will go out of their way to support leaders who they think support them.

CHAPTER 6

Developing Human Capital

E very organization in industry is looking for a competitive advantage. There are many strategies for securing that advantage, but the only true, lasting, competitive advantage an organization has lies in the talents and passion of its people. In this chapter we will focus on how to develop human capital. Specifically, we will focus on the following concepts:

❐ Discussing the importance of leading "persons"
❐ Leveraging people's unique talents and strengths
❐ Engaging the whole person
❐ Focusing on people's strengths
❐ Effectively recruiting, retaining, and developing people
❐ Providing people with a career-changing experience
❐ Recognizing and rewarding success

Many have implemented new processes or technologies in the hope of getting a leg up on the competition. But we live in a copycat world. In the 2009 football season, the Miami Dolphins unveiled a new wrinkle against the New England Patriots—the "wildcat" formation. It seemed to catch the Patriots by surprise and helped Miami win this contest. Within two weeks, every team in the NFL had its own version of the "wildcat" package in its offensive game plan. Was this really a competitive advantage?

Well, it was for a very short period of time. There are very few long-term competitive advantages in any industry. We all have access to the same data, technology, markets, and processes. I would suggest that the only real competitive advantage any organization has is the talents and passion of its people.

Leading "Persons"

On a number of occasions, I have been interviewed by reporters for articles in their trade journals. More than once I have been asked, "How do you lead people?" I always provide the same answer. You don't lead people—you lead persons! Although I am sure that this is grammatically incorrect (being from Brooklyn, a lot of my statements are!), it is critically important to understand.

People are not sheep! To suggest that there is a "one-size-fits-all" approach to leading people is to ignore the unique qualities, dreams, aspirations, and gifts of each individual. Let me use a trite example. I once saw a friend try to "lead" and "motivate" his two children to act a certain way. The carrot/stick he used was to share with his boys, "If you don't behave, we're not going to the circus." Well, this did the trick for son number one, who immediately jumped to attention! However, son number two continued on his path of destruction! After the melee had ended and everyone had cooled down, I asked the younger boy why he hadn't listened to his father. He shared with me, "I hate the circus!" Using the circus as a motivating factor clearly was not a particularly effective approach with this young man.

Too many times we look at people through our own eyes and try to lead them in ways that resonate with us. If we are motivated by money, we think we can get the behaviors we want by holding out cash as an incentive. If we seek glory and recognition, we use these as the tools for getting what we want. I once managed a woman who was a tremendous performer. On several occasions,

I publicly recognized her achievements and asked the team to share their appreciation for her efforts with a round of applause. After the third time I took this approach, she approached me afterward to share with me how uncomfortable public recognition made her feel and asked me to *please* never do that again! Here I was thinking I was showing my appreciation for her fine work, and what I was doing was actually a disincentive! In order to lead "persons," you need to know who they are as unique human beings. You need to know what makes them tick and what you can provide that matters to them.

Many times, people will tell me, "I have too many people to manage to take this approach." I certainly can understand this concern. Many leaders are responsible for leading large groups of people. A CEO of a Fortune 500 company can't possibly know tens of thousands of her employees on a personal basis. On some level, they need to reach out to people "en masse." However, it is critical that they at least make the effort to know their direct reports well enough to take a personalized approach and require that those people take the same approach down the line. Somewhere in the organization, employees must feel that someone cares about them as a human being. Otherwise they will do what they need to do to get by and you may never get the best they have to offer. Marcus Buckingham and Curt Coffman in their outstanding book *First Break All the Rules* speak about the focus of great managers. They identify six important questions that are at the core of successful organizations where people feel valued:[1]

1. Do I know what is expected of me at work?
2. Do I have the materials and equipment I need to do my work right?

---

[1] Marcus Buckingham and Curt Coffman, *First Break All the Rules* (New York: Simon and Schuster, 1999).

3. At work, do I have the opportunity to do what I do best every day?

4. In the last seven days, have I received recognition or praise for doing good work?

5. Does my supervisor, or someone at work, seem to care about me as a person?

6. Is there someone at work who encourages my development?

Can you see some common threads in these questions? Take note that half of these questions relate to having someone in a leadership position know me and care about me as a person, recognize my efforts, and encourage my development. This is simple but powerful stuff.

Leveraging People's Unique Talents

As a sports fan, I am always fascinated by the approaches coaches take to developing high-performing teams. On more than one occasion, I have seen coaches bring in "their system" and try to get the team to adapt to it. As a long-suffering fan of the New York Jets, I recently watched as the team tried to adapt to a new coach who was a proponent of a "3-4" defensive scheme. The problem with this approach was that the personnel on the team had been recruited for, and were better suited to, a "4-3" defensive scheme. It was painful watching players who had spent years trained to play on the line trying to play from a standing position, and vice versa. The results were not good. The Jets wound up deciding to keep this system and simply trade the players who couldn't adapt to it. They hired free agents who were better suited to play in this scheme. A year later, they fired their coach! Most leaders in a corporate setting don't necessarily have the luxury of making "wholesale" changes to personnel simply to fit their scheme.

I was also fortunate enough to see a different type of leadership exhibited by Pat Riley. Many of you probably remember Pat

Riley from his days as the coach of the NBA champion Los Angeles Lakers. Back in the 1980s, the Lakers and Celtics battled every year for the NBA championship, with both teams taking home the trophy multiple times. The Lakers were famous for playing a type of game that became known to basketball fans as *Showtime*. They had incredibly gifted and fluid athletes such as Magic Johnson, James Worthy, and Kareem Abdul-Jabbar. They ran a fast-paced type of basketball that was incredibly fluid and beautiful to watch. It was like ballet on the hardwood!

A number of years later, Pat Riley became the coach of the New York Knicks. He inherited a very different type of team with very different personnel. Instead of having fluid, fast-break "thoroughbreds," the Knicks were more like a team of Clydesdales. They were big, tough, strong, lumbering players. Magic, James, and Kareem had been replaced by Patrick Ewing, Charles Oakley, and Anthony Mason. These were all very talented players— but a very different type of player than the old Lakers teams Riley had coached to championships. As a student of leadership, I was interested in seeing what Riley would do. To his credit, instead of trying to turn the Knicks into something they were not (and were not capable of being!), Riley adapted his approach to the talent and skills he had inherited. He did keep some of the basic tenets of his success (e.g., a focus on good defense), but he allowed the Knicks to play a brand of basketball that played to their strengths. This to me exemplifies great leadership. Riley knew who his players were as people, knew their strengths, and put them in a position to win by playing to their talents.

Engaging the Whole Person

Tell me if you have experienced this scene before. Employees walk into their employer's building. You can almost see them take off their personalities and individualism and check them at the door. They walk into work, and for the next eight to ten hours, they act like drones. They do what they are told to do. They go through the motions working for people who neither recognize nor value their unique talents or attributes. At the end of the day, they punch the proverbial clock (like Fred Flintstone at the Slate Rock and Gravel Company), put their personalities back on, and go back to actually living their lives. What a waste!

For years, there has been a separation between what you do and who you are. As Sheryl Crow put it in her song "We Do What We Can," you work for a living, but try not to confuse it with being alive: "These are the choices we make to survive; you do what you can."[2] Wouldn't it be amazing if you could be yourself in every aspect of your life? What if work was just an extension of who you were and what you had to offer? Now don't get me wrong. Every job has a level of *administrivia,* and certain aspects to it that are less than exciting. However, the more we can tap into people's unique interests, talents, and energy, the greater value we can glean from their engagement. Oh and by the way, the happier, more productive, and more engaged they will be. This is the classic win-win scenario. Yet far too few organizations even attempt to learn about what makes their people tick or how to leverage their individualism for the benefit of the organization.

Through the Lens of the CIO—The Value of Mentoring

When many people think of employee development, they focus on sending their staff to formal training courses and conferences. Although these are certainly valuable development experiences for many people, by no means are they the only way to help develop human capital. One opportunity that many people fail to leverage is the idea of developing mentoring relationships.

---

[2] Sheryl Crow, "We Do What We Can," *Tuesday Night Music Club* (A&M Records, Inc., 1993).

I have been on both sides of this transaction. I have served for many years as a mentor for graduate students at Columbia University's technology management program. I have also served as a group mentor for the CIO Executive Council's Pathways program. In both situations I have gotten as much out of the experience as the people I mentored. You can always learn from someone, regardless of who is the more experienced professional.

I have also had the benefit of having a personal mentor who I worked with at one of my jobs. It was at a time in my career where I was rapidly climbing the corporate ladder. I was seen as a "mover and a shaker" who had a strong reputation for getting things done. I was well liked and respected by my people and my clients. However, I was a bit of a rebel without a cause. When I saw something that I felt was wrong or that needed to be addressed, I became a bit of a zealot in banging on management's door to tell them to develop the intestinal fortitude to deal with these issues. To the people in the organization, this made me something of a cult hero. To the people in my management chain, it made me a pain in the ass!

I worked with a woman who helped me to better understand this dynamic. She taught me how to pick and choose which battles were worth fighting. She helped me to be more analytical about which issues I had the ability to impact and which were lost causes. She helped me to understand that every organization has baggage, and while I should never accept mediocrity, I needed to learn to live in an imperfect world without getting frustrated. Did this make me less passionate or more docile? No, it didn't. But it did help me to mature as a professional and to come across as more even-handed and emotionally intelligent.

The greatest gift you can provide a person is the gift of experience and support. In many cases, you should look outside of

(*continued*)

(*Continued*)

your own organization to find your people-effective mentors. I once set up a woman on my staff with a mentor from our legal department. This woman was a very mature leader who came across in a very buttoned-up and professional manner. She was able to suggest ideas to my staff person to help her be taken more seriously as a leader.

You may even need to go outside of the walls of your company to help your people find suitable mentors. Make sure you help them identify someone who is willing to put in the time and effort and who has exhibited the qualities in their own careers that you are hoping to help develop in your teammate.

Mentoring can be a win-win proposition for all involved if they are willing to invest the effort. As an added bonus, it's free and won't impact your training budget!

Focusing on Strengths

Many of us grew up in corporate America under an interesting development model. The premise of the model was to identify areas where an individual was weak and to work with them to improve in these areas. I am a big believer in human development. I feel that we have an obligation to help the people on our teams grow to their greatest potential. If someone works as a part of my team, I feel I owe them more than just a paycheck for their time and effort. I also believe in human development because I feel that we are all "works in progress" (anyone who has worked with me knows that this is definitely the case for me!). However, the old approach to developing a person's weaknesses makes no sense to me. Let's put it in sporting terms. Let's say you have a seven-foot-tall center on your basketball team who is a great defensive player, and has a great inside game. Why would you work on making this player improve his three-point shooting? At best, even if he works his tail off he will evolve from being a terrible three-point shooter to becoming a mediocre three-point shooter! While this may be a moral victory of sorts, is this the best way to utilize this resource? Is this the best way for this individual to leverage his talents and skills?

I would suggest that great coaches of talent work to people's strengths. Instead of trying to improve an area of weakness, a more effective approach is to leverage a person's talents and put them in positions where they can shine. Perhaps you have a member of your team who is very skilled in customer-facing interactions. She also enjoys these situations and really shines when given these types of opportunities. Then you have another person who is a brilliant technologist but gets hives if he has to talk to management for five minutes! Who do you think you should put in front of your CEO to present on a new initiative? Who do you think you should provide opportunities to present at town hall meetings and conferences? While the answer to these questions may seem apparent, I am always amazed at how little we sometimes leverage our common sense! Please understand that I am not suggesting that you don't deal with a person's weaknesses. This is especially important if a person has a "fatal flaw." For example, it's one thing not to be good in front of a group. It's another to come across so poorly that people will question why the person is even employed! Certainly, you need to help that individual polish his public image. Just don't waste your time and his trying to turn him into Tony Robbins!

Recruiting/Retaining/Developing

I always marvel at how much companies are willing to invest in mergers and acquisitions. These are high-risk endeavors that often do not pay the dividends that are hoped for or expected. These same companies seem unwilling to invest in what is arguably the only real tangible differentiator they have—their people.

To me, an organization's most important asset is its people. Investing the time, effort, and dollars to identify, recruit, develop, and retain your team is the most important investment you will ever make. I always love to hear from HR people that it's dangerous to invest too much in people and make them more marketable because you may lose them. The surest way to lose people is not to develop them and provide them opportunities for growth. Only once in my career did I lose someone because I helped him develop to the point that he outgrew what I could offer him. And God bless him for it! People only owe us to give 100 percent when they are in our employ. They have no obligation to be tied to us for life! I have, however, seen many people leave companies because they were underutilized or not given opportunities to grow, learn, and stretch their wings. I have worked for not-for-profit companies where I could not provide the same level of compensation that other larger local companies could. But I gave these people the opportunity to broaden their skills, their experience, and their contributions. Over the years I haven't lost too many people in this scenario.

You also need to invest a great deal of time and energy ensuring that the people you recruit and hire for your organization have not only the skills and experience they need to be successful but—perhaps even more importantly—also the cultural fit and mentality to fit within your organization. I will take someone with "B" level aptitude and an "A" level attitude any day over someone with great skills but an average or bad attitude. You can teach most people technical and business skills. Good luck doing an attitude or culture change overhaul. Give me someone with desire and a great attitude any day and I can coach them to win.

Through the Lens of the CIO—If you Aren't Teaching Your People, Who Is, and What Are They Teaching Them?

Many of the lessons we learn in life have been learned by watching people in positions of authority. Whether this was your mother teaching you how to be kind or your high school hockey coach teaching you how to be a better teammate, we often pick up our cues and our mores from the leaders we look up to.

As a CIO, whether you realize it or not, your people are constantly looking at you. They are looking for your reaction when the stuff hits the fan. They are looking to see how you handle adversity and how you handle success. They are watching how you interact with the CEO, and maybe more importantly, how you interact with the receptionist.

I am reminded of a commercial that aired a few years ago. Charles Barkley, a great basketball player and an even bigger personality, had a sneaker commercial where he espoused that he was *not* a role model! Well, whether Charles or any other athlete signed up to be or not, by their visibility in the public eye, by default they become role models for our children. And whether you like it or not, you are a de-facto role model for the people on your team.

All of us want to learn from someone who has been down the road before and has the scars to show for it. Like it or not, that's how your people view you. If you aren't willing to establish the "rules of the road" and tell your people how you feel they should play the game, then you are leaving them to their own devices to find other role models. I liken this to parents who are unwilling to discuss delicate topics with their children and to impart their moral standards of how to treat others. If you aren't willing to have the "sex talk" with your kids, then they will learn about sex and how to treat the opposite sex from people like their friends who are far less qualified (but ever so willing)

(continued)

(*Continued*)

to give them advice. They may also not share your code of ethics about how to treat the opposite sex with respect and deal with them as people rather than objects!

This may be a strange metaphor for some of you, but I feel it is an appropriate one. Although our people are certainly not our children (and shouldn't be treated as children!) they are "impressionable" and will take cues from others who they view to be in positions of power or influence. As you look around your company, are you willing to leave this responsibility to other leaders who may or may not share your sense of urgency or ethics? I want my people to constantly think the following questions whenever they encounter a challenge or a difficult interaction: "What would Larry do? What would he want me to do? How do we as an organization deal with people and issues?" If not you, then who?

Making Sure a Person Is Better Off for Having Had the Experience

As I previously stated, although some managers are fearful of losing good employees if they provide too much training or developmental opportunities, we owe the people on our teams the opportunity to grow and develop so that they are better off and more fully rounded as people and professionals for having been a part of our organization.

I feel very strongly about this. Most people who leave an organization don't leave because they have had too many opportunities to develop and grow. They leave because they have had too few! Not only is developing a person the responsibility of a leader, but when you help develop your people, you are also a beneficiary of their increased capacity to contribute. You can leverage their expanded skills for the benefit of the larger team. This is a win-win scenario.

The other flaw in this thinking is that the role of a leader is to keep the same people in the same positions for as long as it serves you. Not only is this selfish, but it is also flawed thinking. In every person's evolution, there comes a time when all parties concerned are better off if the person moves on. You should always provide people with expanded opportunities to contribute as they develop their skills. However, at a certain point, you may not be able to provide individuals with the next level of challenge that is appropriate for their professional development. At that point, the best thing is to wish them well as they move on to the next chapter in their career. You have not only gotten the benefit of their acumen and effort for their time in your employ, but you have gotten the satisfaction of helping them develop and grow.

Both parties should feel good about the fact that their wings are now strong enough to fly out of the nest. This type of turnover is not a sign of weak leadership but of great leadership. How many corporate CEOs have been developed while they were a part of General Electric? How many NFL head coaches learned under the tutelage of Bill Walsh? As we will discuss later in the book, great leaders develop more great leaders.

Recognizing and Rewarding Your People's Efforts and Successes

Every human being wants to be recognized and rewarded. William James stated, "The deepest principle in human nature is the craving to be appreciated." As Henry David Thoreau eloquently stated, "The mass of men live lives of quiet desperation."[3] This is even more pronounced for people who toil in endeavors such

---

[3] Laurence J. Peter, *Peter's Quotations: Ideas for Our Time* (New York: Bantam Books, 1980), 305. Quoted from Henry David Thoreau, "Economy," Walden (originally published Boston: Ticknor and Fields, 1854).

as IT. In many ways, working in IT can feel like a thankless job. When things go well 99 percent of the time—well, isn't that what you get paid for? When they go wrong the other 1 percent, you are called on the carpet. Most of the people in the ranks of your management neither understand what you really do nor appreciate the complexity of something as simple as "keeping the lights on." Therefore, expecting a whole lotta love (with my apologies to Jimmy Page and Robert Plant) isn't very realistic. How many times have you accomplished something outstanding only to have the accomplishment totally overlooked? How did that feel? As a leader, it is critical to remember these feelings and to ensure that your people don't feel them.

Recognition and appreciation manifest themselves differently for each human being. Therefore, it is very important to know what makes each individual tick and to provide them the type of recognition and reward that will be meaningful and motivate them. For some people, formal public recognition is a wonderful thing. They bask in the glow of being recognized in front of their peers and having their accomplishments trumpeted in public. For some people, this type of public attention will make them want to crawl under a rock and hide! Many people feel the best reward and recognition for an outstanding job is the opportunity to take on a more important and challenging project. They thrive on the excitement and challenge of tackling big and thorny issues. The best way to show them your appreciation is to allow them the opportunity to tackle the next issue. There are people who are motivated by having the opportunity to learn and grow as professionals. For them, the best reward is the chance to be exposed to new ideas and subjects. Sending these people to training or providing them a chance to contribute in a totally new way is the best reward. Some people crave the ability to have a greater impact. Broadening their responsibilities and giving them more ownership for the deliverables of the organization is the best medicine. Finally, some people simply want to be compensated for their efforts. This can get a bit tricky, as we can't always directly tie compensation to accomplishment, but we should strive to create a program that ties compensation to results so as to motivate these individuals to perform at their highest level.

The bottom line in effectively recognizing and rewarding people is to know what they value and to ensure that you as their leader provide them the things that feed their soul. When employees feel recognized and appreciated by a leader, they will knock down walls for them! Do your people feel that level of appreciation from you? Do you feel that level of support from them? If not, what are you doing about it?

Lessons Learned

- The only true, lasting, competitive advantage any organization has is the talents and passion of its people.
- Each individual has unique goals and motivators. You need to learn to work with and lead people one at a time, not en masse!
- Each individual has unique talents. A leader's job is to identify and leverage these skills.
- If you focus on people's strengths, they will succeed. If you focus on their weaknesses, they will fail. Great leaders put people in position to play to their strengths and veer away from their weaknesses.
- As a leader, a critical priority is to recruit, retain, and develop leaders throughout your organization.
- Your responsibility to your staff doesn't end with providing them a paycheck! You owe them the opportunity to have a career-changing experience that makes them better off having worked for you.
- Excellent leaders ensure that their people are recognized and rewarded for their contributions.

CHAPTER 7

Leading the Process of Change

C IOs are often hired to lead significant change efforts. It is rare for a new leadership team to be hired when there is not a need for significant transformation. However most people, regardless of the perceived need, are uncomfortable with change. Oftentimes, even when they recognize that change is required, they are not clear on the concrete steps and processes required to engage in and drive the necessary change.

In this chapter we will identify how to lead the process of change. Specifically, we will focus on the following concepts:

- ❏ Recognizing the discomfort of having to change
- ❏ Selling the need for change
- ❏ Making change personal
- ❏ Approaching change as a standard part of your culture
- ❏ Building community
- ❏ Ensuring buy-in
- ❏ Breaking change into pieces
- ❏ Supporting your team's progress
- ❏ Celebrating and communicating success
- ❏ Comparing position versus influence
- ❏ Discussing project and process management
- ❏ Developing a culture of innovation
- ❏ Maintaining accountability

Change Is Uncomfortable

I once heard someone joke that the only people who like change are babies! Human beings are creatures of habit. We like to live in our comfort zone even when it might not feel comfortable anymore.

When I first got married, my wife and I moved into our first apartment in Queens, New York. I started taking mass transportation into Manhattan every day and started seeing the same faces on the bus each morning. One of the people I met was a nice man who lived on my block. He worked for a bank in lower Manhattan and we soon hit it off and began to become friends. As I got to know him better, he began to share with me his level of unhappiness at work. He felt boxed into a dead-end job in an organization that didn't recognize or appreciate his talents. Now, anyone who knows me will tell you that I am a person of action. If you come to me with a problem, my focus is to try and fix it (a quality that has not always served me well in my marriage!). So naturally, when my friend started sharing his unhappiness with me, I went into "fix-it" mode. My first response was that I was pretty good with pulling together resumes and that I would be happy to help him update his. He thanked me for my offer but never took me up on it. A couple of weeks (and many negative job conversations!) later, I offered that I knew some people in executive search and perhaps I could introduce him to their counterparts who focused on financial positions. Once again, he thanked me but never took me up on my offer. After about three months of this back and forth, I finally came to realize that he really didn't want my help. As a matter of fact, he really didn't want anybody's help! What he wanted was someone to whine to about how miserable his job was. Now, 25 years later, I realize that as a friend I should have just smiled and listened, and that this in and of itself would have added value for him. Being young and lacking any finesse at the time, I simply shared with him my observation that he clearly didn't want to change things and asked if we could talk about other topics. (I wasn't a very patient or supportive individual back then! I'm still working on it today.)

The bottom line is that change is uncomfortable. Even when there is compelling motivation for people to change, they still have a hard time building up the intestinal fortitude and energy required for change. (The extra 20 pounds around my midsection would seem to validate that!) Inertia is a very strong force. Building up enough energy to break through its walls is difficult. Therefore, to get people to change, you must be able to motivate them as to the need for change.

Selling the Need for Change

No matter how obvious it may be to you, not everyone will instantly recognize and embrace the need for change. Even in organizations that are struggling, people often resist change. After all, they have worked for years in the current climate. They know the game and how to play it. You can be perceived as a threat to them. You are someone who is trying to rock the boat! You want to make their lives uncomfortable.

The other challenge you may face is that others before you may have failed at bringing successful change to the organization. When I started my current position, three people had occupied my office over the prior five years. It was a revolving door of discontent, both for the people in my seat and the clients these people were trying to support. When I came in, I tried to meet with many of the key executives and stakeholders. Some of them were very reluctant to waste any time on me. After all, I was just the latest in a long string of "flavors of the day." If they waited long enough, I would go away, just like the rest had before me. This was also true for the staff I inherited. Why should they jump through hoops to accommodate my plans when they were more likely to be here in a year than I was?

A leader must be able to sell the need for change. Regardless of the situation, you must help people understand why the status quo is not an acceptable option and how failure to change will impact them. Note that I said impact *them,* not impact the organization. Some people may not care if the walls crumble around them as long as they can stay in place. Leaders must be able to vividly describe the consequences of a failure to change to each individual in the organization. They must also be able to articulate the upside of change for the individuals who are being asked to change.

Personalizing the Need for Change

Whenever someone tries to "sell" us something (like the need for change), each of us has the same question in mind: "What's in it for me?" It is imperative that you make an effort to know the people you hope to lead and influence (not only your own staff by the way) and individualize for each of them an answer to this question. For some people, the answer might be that changing will allow them to grow into greater opportunity and challenge. For others, changing might allow them to continue on with the organization and provide continued stability and employment. For others, change might create a platform to enhance their visibility within the organization and allow them to be recognized for their contributions. Regardless of what the motivators are, you need to find out what matters to each person and appeal to their individual interests.

Making Change a Part of Your Culture

One of the biggest misconceptions people have is that change is a one-time deal. Many of us have lived through the organizational approach of the day. Over the years there have been countless books and approaches to improving organizations, and we have all lived through these various approaches— whether it be Six Sigma or SLAs for everything from new innovations to falling out of trees and hoping we are caught by our colleagues. Many of these management strategies have some real value in their messages and lessons. However, the one problem that any approach has is that it leaves people with the perspective that once this is over, we can get back to normal.

When I worked in the pharmaceutical industry, I had a colleague who we'll call George. George was a brilliant technologist and one of the smartest people I have ever met. But George was not a big fan of change. He was extremely set in his ways and resistant to trying any new approaches. Time after time, we would be dealing with new and more challenging issues. Instead of viewing this as the nature of business, each time he viewed the issue as a "one-off" anomaly. His famous line, which he used constantly, was, "This is all well and good, but when things go back to normal. . . ." After hearing this comment a couple of dozen times, I finally said to him, "George, this *is* the new normal! We will never go back to how things were before."

The very definition of *normal* suggests how things are the majority of the time. Well, things are always in flux. Therefore, change is the one constant you can count on. In essence, change is the new normal. Giving people the idea that they have to be flexible and willing to change for a short and finite period of time sets a false expectation and does them a great disservice. People need to understand that the only way to succeed in the new world order is to learn to embrace change instead of looking for ways to avoid it.

This is sometimes a scary message to deliver (or to hear), but it must be ingrained in everyone's subconscious if we are to succeed in the twenty-first century. Those of us who grew up as part of the baby boomer generation were sold a bill of goods that sounded something like this: You work hard to get a good education. You find a good company that will hire you. You work for 30 years as a loyal member of that company. You retire with a gold watch and a nice pension, buy a condo down in Boca Raton, and play golf with your cronies until you fade into the sunset. Sound familiar? Fortunately, the generations that have come after us have no delusions of this nature.

The days of someone or some company "taking care of you" are a thing of the past. Companies today are more focused on making the next quarter than worrying about their people for the next 20 years. Like it or not, you are the captain of your own destiny. For many of us, this is actually a liberating and empowering realization. Once you know you are at the helm, you are free to take the chances and actions you deem necessary for success.

It's important for your team to understand that once you embark on a transformational effort, you have hit the point of no return. You will never be the same. Things will never go back to normal. And that's a good thing! If you look at nature, everything that is alive is either growing and evolving or dying. Nothing remains stagnant. The competition changes, the landscape changes, expectations and reality change. The IT industry is littered with the ghosts of companies who were first-to-market industry leaders but who unfortunately did not evolve with the marketplace and are now the stuff of history (does anyone remember Digital Equipment Corporation or token ring?). As a leader, you have to get people to not only come to grips with but also eventually to embrace the fact that change is constant. This creates great opportunity for growth, evolution, and development, and ensures that life is never boring. It keeps us agile and sharp.

I can't imagine working in an environment where your tasks, clients, or objectives never change. Many people are attracted to careers in IT based on the allure of ever-changing technologies and solutions. We need to take that same enthusiasm for progress and apply it to our organizations.

Through the Lens of the CIO—Can the CIO be an Organizational Change Agent?

Many people question the impact a CIO can have on the overall organization. Sure, he can improve the IT function. He may even be able to transform the department into a value-driven business partner. But can he really have an impact on the overall company? Here's why I think he can!

First of all, with the exception of the CEO, no other corporate executive has such a broad purview as the CIO. CIOs are uniquely qualified to see across every part of the organization. They can see how processes intertwine, how people collaborate, how one business process impacts another, and how the entire lifecycle from conception of an idea to delivering a product or service comes to be. There is enormous power in having a macro view of the company and the industry it functions within that, if correctly leveraged, can lead to strategic differentiation.

Second, we live in a world where information is king and technology drives consumer behavior. The days of IT being something that happened inside glass walls and was parceled out to "users" is a thing of the past. Most teenagers carry around more computing power in their pockets than we had running corporations just a few decades ago. Consumers expect access to everything from everywhere. People cannot function without their iPhones or Blackberries. Technology has been woven into every aspect of life in the twenty-first century, and no one better understands how to leverage this reality than the CIO.

The way we conduct business and do marketing and advertising has changed in a revolutionary way. People spend more time on Facebook than they do reading newspapers. More of today's news is digested from blogs and websites than from listening to Katie Couric or Brian Williams (sorry, guys!). You can reach a broader audience from a Twitter account than you can

(continued)

(*Continued*)

from a front page on *USA Today*. We TiVo shows so we can skip the television commercials. Packaged and consumer goods companies are eliciting online suggestions for new products and using consumers as their think tanks. Want to conduct a focus group? Put up an online survey and you will have thousands of valid data points in less than a day. More people visit Google for answers than ever stepped into a library. If you don't believe me, just watch your kids do research for their book reports!

If you look at the capital budgets of most organizations, technology-related business initiatives have the lion's share. Business analytics are helping to drive better, more timely decisions on what markets to enter, what products to create, and what audiences to target to consume these products. No other group understands program and project management better than IT. No other group has more of a global reach and has to support a more diverse client community than IT. No one is better positioned to understand how to leverage social media, how to use technology to get your message across, or how to engage consumers of your products and services than the CIO.

Still wonder if the CIO can act as an organizational change agent?

Building Community

In my experience, there is an enormous difference between what I will call groups and what we think of as teams. Groups are a collection of people who are brought together because of a common skill set or function. Teams, by contrast, are a collection of committed, like-minded people who have dedicated themselves to a common purpose. This is not semantics—it is much more powerful than that. One of the main differences between groups and teams is the concept of *community*.

Building community is a critical part of developing and leading an effective team. People want to feel connected to a purpose they believe in. They also want to feel a connection to each other. As a leader, your role is to build within people a sense of common identity and purpose that makes them feel a part of something bigger than themselves. One step in accomplishing this objective is to allow people with common beliefs to gravitate toward each other and work together toward a common purpose. This is a natural evolution that will happen without a great deal of outside interference. The tougher approach is to get people with diverse ideas and beliefs to band together. The best way to accomplish this is to create a higher purpose or objective for which people are willing to put aside their personal agendas to work toward.

Ensuring Buy-in

Having their minds is not enough to be successful. In order to get the results you need, you need to have their hearts and souls. Too many people go to work, leave their energy, creativity, and passion at the door, punch the clock, put in their ten hours, and pick up their real selves on the way out the door at night. This may be enough if you are trying to tread water. But driving large-scale change requires more. It requires a level of energy, passion, enthusiasm, and resiliency that only comes when the people involved have bought into the need for and value of the articulated change.

I had a person who worked for me in a prior job who was possibly the most brilliant and talented individual I have ever known. This individual understood the value of the Internet before any of us even knew what WWW stood for (back then, it meant World Wide Wrestling to me!). He was creative, innovative, and ahead of his time. Unfortunately, he was also a rogue who never aligned with the decisions and directions of the organization. If the team aligned behind a certain technology standard that he didn't agree with, he would "recommend" a different solution to the clients. Ultimately, in spite of his acumen, talents, and brilliance, he was let go because he never bought into or supported what the team was trying to accomplish.

It is critical to ensure that people understand why you are asking them to take a certain action, see the value of that decision both for them as well as the clients who are impacted, and have an emotional stake in the outcome. Going through the motions is not enough. You need your people to help evangelize, motivate, and drive change. No matter how many homilies you deliver from the pulpit, they won't mean a hill of beans unless the people on your team are embracing the messages you are espousing.

Breaking Change into Bite-sized Chunks

Change is scary for everyone. Breaking through the barrier of inertia is a significant challenge to implementing the required changes to an organization. Most people feel frozen and immobilized when faced with broad, large-scale change imperatives. Looking at the entirety of what is required to overhaul an organization can be very intimidating. People can easily feel overwhelmed by what they see as too large a row to have to hoe. That's why it is crucial to communicate the need for change in an incremental way and provide smaller milestones along the path. I am reminded of the old joke, "How do you eat an elephant?" The answer, of course, is, "One bite at a time!" Breaking change into manageable chunks gives people the confidence that they can accomplish what is required. It also allows for success along the way, which further motivates people to stay the course and continue down the path of long-term change.

Supporting Progress along the Way

Transformation can be a long journey. Asking people to change and asking them to do things that may be uncomfortable for extended periods of time is at best a risky proposition. You need to approach preparing for and managing a transformation in a fashion that is very similar to dealing with a marathon. You would never show up and expect to run the Boston or New York City Marathon without having trained for months. You would have started a training regimen and slowly, over time, extended your runs until they start to approach the distance of the race. You would rest between workouts and refuel with a healthy diet. And once you arrive at the race, you would never try to run a marathon as if it were a hundred-yard dash!

Many leaders don't take the time and planning required to manage a transformation effort appropriately. In their zeal, they run their people as if the race was a dash. They talk about the finish line in order to motivate people, but the finish line can appear too far off in the distance to have a positive impact. As a matter of fact, it can become a demoralizing milestone, since it is impossible to see until you are very close. Golfers on a par-five hole know that they have to select various targets along the course in order to hit or break par. There is no way a golfer can set her sights on the pin when you are 400 to 500 yards from the hole. You must focus on targets and milestones along the way. Transformations must be addressed in a very similar fashion. You must select milestones that are achievable and in close enough view that people can see them and believe they are achievable. You must also ensure that you are encouraging people along the way, reminding them of why they are expending such great effort and doing things that might at first seem unnatural and uncomfortable.

Many parents know that when trying to teach their children a new skill, there are certain behaviors they need to exhibit.

The first of these is modeling. In many cases, the best way to teach someone how to acquire a new skill is to show them how to do it effectively. This is important not only as a teaching tool but also because it is critical for people to see you doing the things you are espousing. The second thing many parents do is to praise or reward their children when they approximate success. You cannot expect someone who is performing a new skill to do so perfectly the first time out of the gate. It takes practice and trial and error. When you see your people straining to do something uncomfortable, you need to recognize and reward the effort and let them know when they are making progress on a continuum. If you wait for perfection to reward them, it may never come. When someone does something "approximately" correct, give them a pat on the back.

People tire during any marathon. There are crucial points when people decide whether they will choose to soldier on or whether they crumble under the strain of the effort. It is important to allow people to take an occasional break. It's OK to slow down every now and then. It's not OK to stop. Breaking inertia is a huge challenge. Make sure that people recharge and rest a bit along the way but never allow them to get derailed because starting from a stalled position is a recipe for failure. You often see runners grab a cup of water or an energy drink from stations along the road, without missing a stride. Make sure you are there for your people with your own brand of "energy drink" to keep them motivated, focused, and headed in the right direction.

Celebrating and Communicating Progress/Success

I am the epitome of the stereotypical Type-A New Yorker. I talk fast, I walk fast, I think fast (although not always clearly!). I am very results-oriented and focused on checking things off of my to-do list. In my world, success is all about getting things done and moving on to the next challenge. I don't expect a lot of fanfare and recognition (which is a good thing, because few of us get it that often!). Although this is who I am as a person, it is a terrible approach to handling people engaged in a significant transformation effort.

There are two critical things an effective transformational leader must ensure that she does as part of her efforts. The first is to celebrate success. When I speak of success, I'm not only referring to the end result of a two-year effort but, more importantly, also to accomplishing the important milestones along the way. We talked about the fact that fatigue can set in as part of any major long-term effort. We also discussed how easy it is to lose track of the goal or get disheartened along the path. As a leader, you must ensure that your team takes the time and effort to celebrate intermediate successes on the road to your longer-term objective. This can be as simple as publicly recognizing the team at a town hall meeting or as part of your ongoing client communiqué. It can be as low-key as bringing in a few pizzas and taking 30 minutes to celebrate. It's not about how much you spend or how glitzy the celebrations. It's all about making people know that you appreciate their progress and that they have made inroads toward the larger goals. The two most underutilized words in the English language are "thank you."

Associated with celebrating success is the need to communicate progress. We already discussed the need for marketing the value of IT in a previous chapter. For example, perhaps when you committed to your board of directors that you would transform your organization, you laid out an 18-24-36 month program. What indications have they been given along the way that you are making headway? How do they know if things are progressing according to, ahead of, or behind schedule? How do they know the impact of your team's efforts if you don't communicate them? It is imperative for a leader to constantly communicate incremental progress so that he or she doesn't lose the confidence, funding, support, or goodwill from the key stakeholders you need to accomplish your mission. Once again, the objective here is not how sexy the communication is but that you are keeping people apprised of your progress and helping them understand what's in it for them. I have seen too many people have the rug (or budget) pulled out from under them because some sexier initiative became more front and center on the executive radar screen and they lost the support and momentum they needed to get to the end game. There is a reason why teams are given first downs in football and not expected to get the ball into the end zone on four plays—the same is true in business.

Through the Lens of the CIO—What If the Rest of the Company Won't Change?

Lots of people get frustrated because they feel that other people or parts of their organizations "don't get it." Perhaps you are fortunate enough to work for a high-performance IT organization. What good is it, you think to yourself, for us to be excellent when the folks in research and development are mediocre and our salesforce stinks? It's easy to get despondent and allow complacency and mediocrity to creep into your bloodstream. Here's why you shouldn't do it.

Each of us has a professional responsibility to bring our best to the job. Regardless of how anyone else is playing the game, you need to perform at a high level. One important reason for this is your own personal integrity. Once you lose your integrity, you've lost everything. What would happen if you started to come back to the pack and became mediocre like you perceive everyone else to be? You have to decide in life whether you plan to be part of the solution or part of the problem. Besides, if the organization is truly mediocre, one of two things could happen. One, you lose your job because the company is taking on water. Two, you decide to leave because it's a frustrating place to work. What happens when you have to find, and work at, your next job? If you have allowed the insidious disease of "who cares" to creep into your thinking and work ethic, you either won't find another job (because this comes through in your interviews) or you won't succeed in your next job because you have become one of those people you used to complain about!

What if you decide you want to stay at your company and try to make a difference? Wouldn't you like to see things change? Well, how do you think change happens? Do you think one day someone waves a magic wand and all the frogs are transformed into princes and princesses? No, change is an incremental process that happens in phases over time. One group starts to improve and this starts to rub off on another. People see how you are playing the game and have to run faster to keep up with you. Just the same way mediocrity can be contagious, so can greatness. I'm a fan of the New York Mets (a difficult admission to make!). The Mets last won the World Series in 1986. But they started to win the battle in 1984 when they traded for Keith Hernandez. They infused a winning player with a winning attitude and leadership qualities into their clubhouse. This was the start of a turnaround from being a joke of a team to being world champions. Transformation has to start somewhere—why not start with you? Why not start with IT? We already talked about how pervasive the reach of IT is and how visible its impact can be in an organization. Why can't IT lead the way to organizational transformation?

Finally, I always share with my people the following thought. Even if we wind up being on the *Titanic,* we will make sure that our deck chairs are lined up! I am a big believer in personal accountability and being able to shave the guy staring back at me in the mirror. You owe it to yourself and to the people you lead to play at a high level, care at a high level, and invest every ounce of acumen and energy you have to make a difference. OK—I'll get off the soapbox now!

Comparing Position versus Influence

The final piece of the puzzle regarding leading the change effort is the fact that effective leadership and change are rarely driven based on position. They are normally driven by influence. I always tell people that you may have deference to an office, but respect for the individual in that office has to be earned. We have all seen organizations where there are people with fancy titles in big offices who have no clue as to what is really going on while individual contributors know the real deal. We have often seen executive assistants be able to get things done and know what strings to pull to drive outcomes. Their effectiveness was not based on a fancy title but on their influence with key people within and outside the organization.

I saw this up close and personal in my life. My mother was a very simple woman who never held an executive position, never made a lot of money, and never made the front page of the newspaper. However, based on her kindness and influence, she was loved, respected, and able to get things done that business leaders and politicians could not. When she passed away, there was a line of mourners so long that the funeral parlor had to close down all the other chapels in order to handle the overflow! People on the outside wanted to know who this woman was. She wasn't famous, or rich, or powerful in the normal sense of those words. She was a person of great influence, not based on position or title but based on character, personality, and personal attributes.

It is important to remember that your title may get you a bit down the road to success, but you will never accomplish your long-term objectives unless you develop the ability to influence people and decisions for which you don't have direct impact or responsibility.

It is also important to identify the members of your team, as well as your peers who hold influence within the organization and work to elicit their support and alignment for your goals. Success is a team sport. No one ever scored a touchdown without a lot of people blocking for them. There is a reason why all-pro quarterbacks buy their linemen Rolexes! Understanding and leveraging influence is an important part of that process.

Balancing Change with Disciplined Project Management

One of the major issues I have faced in driving transformation efforts has been creating an appropriate balance between the need for nimbleness and the requirement for a disciplined approach to project management. Most organizations seem to struggle getting themselves into this sweet spot.

When I arrived at my current position, the environment I inherited reminded me of the wild, wild West! There was no project management methodology in place. As a matter of fact, there was not even a project approval process. My predecessor would receive a pot of money at the beginning of each year with no real focus on how to use it. People would line up outside his office like a pastry shop asking for money. It was first come, first served. When the money ran out, the money ran out. Needless to say, projects (if you want to call them that) were never completed on time or on budget. There was no apparent value to how money was being spent (notice I said *spent,* not invested). The first time I met our chairman of the board he shook my hand and said, "Larry, IT is a black hole where money goes in and nothing of value comes out." Obviously, this was not an auspicious beginning. The project management process was broken.

A More Disciplined Approach

One of the first things we put in place was a governance process for project consideration. First of all, we stated that there would be no more IT projects. People of course looked at me like I had three heads. How could there be no IT projects? What I explained to both my board as well as the key executives of the organization was that all projects needed to have a business purpose, with stated and measurable business value. I also shared that they needed to be sponsored by a business leader (for those of you who are thinking, "Hey, what about infrastructure projects?" I act as the business sponsor for those). This was a new approach and took some time to take root.

At first, business executives were not comfortable acting as the voice and face of the project. I assured them that my team and I would work with them to develop a project charter, identify the ROI and business value of the proposed effort and help them develop the sales pitch to the board of directors. I also let them know that members of their team would have to have skin in the game. They needed to "own" the project and invest the time and effort to help shepherd it to successful completion. In the past, they had launched ideas over the wall to IT and didn't reengage until the project was "completed." As you can imagine, there were not a lot of happy clients. They would look at what IT had built and say that's not what I wanted, or that's not what I meant. Since they had no accountability for the outcomes, what would follow was a finger-pointing exercise where everyone lost and IT looked bad. With the new process, everyone was accountable so people had a vested interest in making sure that only projects that added real value were considered and that they were engaged throughout the process.

We also put a three-tiered governance process in place. Step one was to vet out the value of the projects as well as the approach and associated costs with key financial and technology "experts" throughout the organization. If the project passed muster with them, it was then put in front of our budget committee. Only if the projects passed both of those gauntlets was it even considered by the board of directors for funding approval. The first year we did this, I wound up doing most of the talking at the board meeting, in spite of the fact that the business sponsors were supposed to be the voice of the projects. After a couple of years, I found myself in the room simply for moral support or to explain any technical details. The business sponsors were totally accountable for selling the ideas and accepting joint responsibility with me for the outcome of the projects. Needless to say, our success rate was positively impacted by this approach.

Another aspect of project discipline beyond governance is the actual methodology of project management. In some organizations, the culture is mature enough to implement Six Sigma black belts. Most organizations are not necessarily ready for this level of discipline, nor for the required level of capital investment. In my company, we rolled out what I lovingly refer to as *PMI Light*. It has all of the major pillars of the Project Management Institute methodology but is simple and lightweight enough for our clients to embrace without feeling intimidated or encumbered. Clients are co-owners of each project and are involved from the genesis of developing a project proposal to the post-rollout operational checkpoint. There is a shared sense of accountability, and people literally feel like these are their projects—because they are!

What has been the impact of this approach? Well, first of all, frivolous projects never see the light of day and are shot down well before they get to be considered by the board of directors. Our success rate for delivering projects on time, on budget and on value is 100 percent for eight consecutive years. Compare that to the industry average of 34 percent project success as articulated by the Standish Group. That means that fully two thirds of every IT project fails to deliver on their promises. We no longer have that problem.

Process as Disabler

I would like to share one cautionary tale regarding project and process discipline. One of my managers in a prior life latched onto process management with a vigor bordering on fanaticism. Whenever a client wanted to do something, they were told they had to follow the process. Any slight deviation from process and the client could not pass go or collect $200. Well, the whole idea of process management is to be able to create repeatable and successful outcomes. There are times when your process might be too rigid or be in need of reengineering. I would strongly suggest that you occasionally revisit your processes along with your clients and elicit their feedback regarding what works for them in the real world and what frustrates them. Armed with this knowledge, adapt your processes to the culture and environment you are working in. The only thing worse than having no process discipline is having things so narrowly defined that no one can get anything accomplished! Remember, you are there to serve a client community, so figure out how your processes can best accomplish this objective.

Developing a Culture of Innovation

One of the hottest topics in the industry the past few years has been the need for innovation. You hear a lot about how being able to innovate is a key differentiator in today's competitive marketplace. Much of the focus is on formal processes for innovation, setting aside specific budgets to create innovation sandboxes, and developing formal teams and processes to drive creativity. This is all well and good, but to me this isn't the biggest challenge to developing an innovative organization.

In my mind, the number one variable in ensuring that your organization can leverage effective innovation is creating a culture of innovation. Let me describe what that means to me and also compare and contrast it with what I see in many organizations.

These are difficult economic times. We are navigating through what many have described as the most challenging economic climate since the Great Depression. Whether you want to refer to it as a recession, a depression, or Armageddon, the bottom line is that money is tight and every company out there is focused on the bottom line and on making its next quarter. In this type of environment, it is difficult to accept mistakes. I have worked in places where I would describe the culture as a *culture of blame*. People do a lot of finger-pointing and punish those who make mistakes. However, innovation is rarely a straightforward process that is successful the first time, every time. Thomas Edison is widely thought to have said regarding the light bulb, "I did not fail. I found 10,000 ways that did not work." In a culture of blame, Edison would have been fired the first day!

There is an old saying that the only way a turtle can make any progress is by sticking out his neck. In order for people to innovate, they have to be willing to take chances and think outside the box. Innovation has many stops and starts and the path to success is rarely a straight line. If you expect your people to be willing to take prudent risks, they have to know that you have their backs! In many environments, the leader takes credit for success and throws others under the bus when things go awry. This cannot be the case if you hope to nurture a culture of innovation. You must allow your people to safely try things that are novel and creative. They have to know that working on the bleeding edge doesn't mean that they are the ones who will be donating the blood!

Developing a Culture of Accountability

In some organizations, people feel that leadership is something that happens *above* them. It is as if they are waiting for Zeus to throw down an edict from Mount Olympus before they take any action. I have been a part of several transformation efforts where people have complained, "I agree with all of this, but my manager doesn't get it." They moan and groan about how they can't impact things because they work for clowns. This mentality infuriates me. I actually responded to one person who told me this by stating, *"Working for a clown doesn't give you license to join the circus!"*

I *am* IT!

One of the most important components for driving meaningful change is to develop a culture of accountability in every single person who is engaged in the process. People need to feel a sense of pride in ownership and that this is their organization. If they feel that leadership is responsibility for the organization's success, then you have a management versus labor mentality that will not succeed. Let me explain this by sharing a little story.

About three weeks into my current role, I happened to be in line in the company cafeteria when I overheard a conversation between one of my clients and a member of my staff. The client was explaining to my staff member that she was having an e-mail-related challenge. His very curt response was, "E-mail is not my problem." Needless to say, he now had a bigger problem—dealing with me! One of the rallying cries that I try to drive into the subconscious of anyone who works with me is that "I *am* IT!" That means that any IT-related problem is, by definition, my problem. When it is an area where I have the expertise and ability to directly impact it, I should. If it's something outside of my area of expertise or my sphere of control, I should (figuratively) walk the clients over to someone on the team who can address their concern. If someone has shared a problem with any member of my team, in essence, he or she has "spoken to IT." We are all accountable for the success of the team. I have seen teams where dissension is the rule of the land. Can you imagine how successful your favorite football team would be if the defense took joy in the offense fumbling the ball? We all have a stake in this game, and we are all part of making things work. If things are going to improve, then I have to help make that happen. Again I say: "I *am* IT!"

Leadership Begins with Me!

You see, in my mind, leadership begins with me! I have had the great fortune to work for some excellent leaders. I have also worked for some less-than-stellar individuals. In both scenarios, the caliber of the person I worked for had nothing to do with the way I was going to lead my team. My responsibility is to make sure that the things I am accountable for work and to try my best to positively affect those things outside of my direct sphere of influence. Working for someone who "doesn't get it" is not an excuse to not get it done. We are all accountable for our actions and for what we bring to the party. Regardless of what your management is doing, you need to do the right thing. You need to be the example for your people to model. Leadership needs to start somewhere. In my opinion, leadership begins with me!

Lessons Learned

- Change is uncomfortable. Left to their own devices, people will not get out of their comfort zones to embrace change.
- Change must be sold to people. You must personalize the value of the change for each individual in terms of both the upside of the requested change as well as the downside of not embracing this change.
- Change must become an expected and standard part of your organizational culture.
- Before launching a major change initiative, you must ensure that you have people's buy-in.
- Transformational change can seem overwhelming. You must break the change into bite-sized chunks.

(continued)

(Continued)

- Make sure that your team has the support it needs to accomplish the expected change.
- It is critical to track, communicate, and celebrate successes on the road to completing the required change.
- Change is the new status quo! Get used to it, embrace it, and make a decision to lead it!
- People get more accomplished through influence than through formal authority or position.
- In order to drive meaningful change, you need to implement and embrace project and process management. However, processes should be adaptable to your clients' needs and realities.
- The biggest incentive to successful innovation is creating a culture where prudent risk taking and occasional missteps are rewarded, not punished.
- Successful change requires everyone to embrace accountability.
- No matter what anyone else above you is doing, leadership begins with you!

CHAPTER 8

Partnering for Success

A nyone who has been in a leadership position for more than a day knows that it's impossible to accomplish much as an individual. This chapter discusses the importance of partnerships in creating success. Specifically, we will focus on the following concepts:

- ❏ Defining partnership
- ❏ Creating an empowered, team-oriented environment
- ❏ Adjusting to the workforce of the twenty-first century
- ❏ Partnering with your team
- ❏ Partnering with your clients
- ❏ Partnering with your executive management and board
- ❏ Outsourcing to expand your team
- ❏ Networking to build industry partnerships

Partnerships are especially important in the world of IT, where there are sub-specialties of specialties requiring great depth of knowledge. The last time I wrote code, it was in Cobol. The last time I designed a network, we deployed intelligent hubs into a new technology that had just come out known as a Cisco AGS router. Needless to say, if you are counting on me to be your technical expert in installing and operating technology, you are in deep trouble. I often smile when I am in the boardroom and when an AV issue occurs, everyone turns to me as if I were the AV geek in high school (no disrespect to those of you who were the AV geek in high school!). In any area of endeavor, it takes a team to accomplish any substantial undertaking.

Some Words Are Used Too Loosely

Have you ever noticed how certain words become in vogue and then start getting used to describe everything under the sun? These days, any guy with three servers in his garage can state that he is running a cloud computing service. One of the words that get bandied about way too loosely and too often for my taste is the word *partnership*. People refer to vendors that they have worked with for a month as a *strategic partner*. Since this chapter is devoted to discussing the need and value of partnerships, I thought I should take the time to at least provide you my definition and frame of reference for what I believe it means to develop a partnership.

Partnerships are not relationships with random people or organizations. You probably work with many vendors but only a few true partners. If I walk into the local deli and order a pound of turkey breast, the owner of the deli is not my partner. He is the guy who sells me my cold cuts. A partner is much more than someone with whom you conduct simple transactions. Partnerships are about a common vision, common objectives, and shared accountability. You will never see a partner point a finger or play the blame game stating that the issue is "not my problem."

Partners are the people who are with you in the foxhole when things look bleakest. They have your back and you have theirs. There is no time or energy spent discussing where the boundaries of responsibility end. All the time and energy is spent locking arms and going to battle together. In IT, especially in the twenty-first century, there are myriad partnerships that an effective CIO needs to develop. I will touch on many of them in the following pages.

Creating an Empowered, Team-oriented Environment

One of the most important things you can do to develop a partnership with your team is to empower team members to drive the outcomes you need to accomplish. If they are simply following orders, they will not have the emotional investment needed to accomplish great things. They need to feel that the decisions that are being made are their decisions and that any success or failure that occurs is a direct reflection on them.

One of the mistakes leaders make is inadvertently pitting their people against each other. They have to vie for dollars, resources, and attention. They are taught that they win and are rewarded as individuals, not as a team. It's easy for groups of people to point fingers. It's much more difficult for *teammates* to take that tack. One example (yes, I like football!) helps bring that point home.

I remember years ago the Tampa Bay Buccaneers, who were coached by Tony Dungy, had the best defense in the NFL. Unfortunately, they also had one of the worst offenses in the league. With a Super Bowl–caliber defense, they should have had more success. It was a credit to their coach's leadership that you never heard a peep from the defense about how badly the offense stunk or the fact that if these guys ever got their act together, they would win a Super Bowl. They functioned as a single unit with no finger pointing or blame. This is a direct result of excellent leadership and a shared vision.

In the case of the Bucs, the best players on the team suffered the fate of obscurity because they were connected with a losing team. The corollary of this premise is that all ships rise with the tide. When a team is empowered to succeed, every member of the team benefits.

The following example pains me as I am a die-hard New York Mets fan (talk about being a glutton for punishment!) and do not root for the Yankees. However, as a student of leadership, I do have to recognize greatness when I see it, and the Yankees have developed a culture of winning and have won more World Series (27) than any other team has won championships in any other sport. In 2009, the Yankees won the World Series. Every member of the team received a beautiful World Series ring. If you look on the finger of Francisco Cervelli, who was the Yankees' backup catcher, you will see the same ring as that worn by Derek Jeter, who is a certain first-ballot Hall of Famer.

You see, while there are no winners on a losing team, there are also no losers on a winning team. So the question you need to ask yourself is whether it's more important for you to be seen as an outstanding individual contributor on a mediocre team or to be a part of a great team, even if that means less personal recognition for you and more for the other members of your team.

Adjusting to the Twenty-first-century Workforce

I was born in 1959, near the tail end of what we have come to know as the baby boomer generation. I was raised at a time when we were taught to respect authority, to be grateful to your employer for giving you a job, and to do as you were told. The fact that I went to Catholic grammar school (I still have flashbacks of nuns rapping my knuckles with a ruler) only further ingrained this mentality. We were led to believe that you found a company to work for, toiled in the proverbial fields for 30+ years, and at the end you received a gold watch, a pension, and the opportunity to wear plaid pants and play the back nine at some golf course in Florida. Somewhere along the way, this scenario evaporated as companies had to make difficult financial decisions, often at the expense of their peoples' benefits.

The days of loyalty to an employee and a company seem in many cases to be a relic of the past.

Today's generation (called many things these days, but I'll stick with millennials) have a very different perspective on their work lives. They feel that they should be recognized and rewarded for their talents. They have grown up in the age of free agency where they are willing to trade their skills to the highest bidder. They feel a sense of entitlement that work is only a part of their lives and that their employer should create the kind of culture where they can have a holistic life experience.

Neither one of these generations are either right or wrong. They simply have a different perspective and set of expectations that they bring to the workplace. Add to this generation X and generation Y and you can see that the workforce of the twenty-first century is far more complex than at any other time in the past. And for good measure, more organizations have become global. Therefore, you also have all of the unique nuances of the various cultures represented by the countries your workforce calls home.

I remember years ago my first experience with global responsibility. I was rolling out a global network for a Fortune 100 pharmaceutical company. Our goal was to implement 75 sites in over 50 countries in less than nine months (this was considered a great accomplishment before the Internet was prevalent in every cow pasture around the world). I called the local telephone company in Italy to discuss an implementation date for our link to Rome. I kindly requested an August 8 install date. I was told that would not be possible. OK . . . I'll play nice—how about August 15? Well, I was told that would also not be possible. When I inquired why I was told that the whole country took off the entire month of August for vacation! Being a Type-A New Yorker, you can imagine how my brain short-circuited with that piece of information. However, I quickly learned that the entire country of Italy was not going to change to accommodate me (even if I do have an Italian surname!). I had to learn to work within the parameters of what would work for that culture. The same holds true today, regardless of what generation or culture you are dealing with. You need to learn the language and nuances of the people you are engaging if you hope to be able to leverage their talents to accomplish your objectives.

Partnering with Your Team

Although there are many important partnerships required for success, none is more important than the bond you develop with your team. It is important for you to market and communicate your visions and your progress, but your words will fall on deaf ears if your own people are not espousing the same values and messages when they are in the field touching your client community day in and day out.

As a leader, nothing gets done unless you have the support of the members of your team. You can probably beat and cajole people to adhering to some principles in the short term, but if they feel that they "work for the man" they will undermine you every chance they get when you are not looking. We talked a little about shared accountability and vision. We talked about empowering people and getting their buy-in for your program. Your team has to have the same sense of urgency, commitment, and passion about the vision you do if you hope to move the chains in any meaningful way. Do your people feel a part of your team? Do they feel that you are even on the same team they are? Do they think of themselves as offensive linemen and you as the general manager sitting in a cozy, glass-enclosed corporate box, or do they see you as the quarterback in the huddle with them, setting up for the next play?

Partnering with Your Clients

Nothing is more divisive than having a confrontational relationship with your clients. Can you imagine running a business where you are embroiled in constant combat with your customers? How long do you think you would survive? I've often stated that while the customers might not always be right, they are always the customers. We work in a service-related industry. Our goal is to help our key stakeholders succeed. Is that how we go about working with people?

I have two pet peeves for which I fine the members of my team. All fines come along with a dollar penalty, which I collect, match, and donate at the end of the year to Autism Speaks (a great organization that does wonderful work with developmentally disabled people; www.autismspeaks.org). The first finable offense is arriving late for a meeting. We have grown up to be a culture where people's personal time is not respected. Although money can be replaced, time cannot. We only have some many hours on this planet, so we should respect our time and the time of the people we work with. The second finable offense is to use what my team has scathingly come to refer to as the "U" word. We refer to the people to whom we provide service as our *clients,* not our *users.* User is a pejorative term that carries negative connotations and emotional baggage. If you think about it, the only other area of endeavor besides IT that refers to the people they service as users is the world of illicit drugs! Language is a powerful thing, and I feel it is important to use it in a positive way.

In many organizations, IT and "the business" are at odds with each other. Neither seems to understand or respect the other. Going back to my premise of all of us being on one team, my people understand that our clients are not separate and discrete from our team. Rather, we all understand that we are all on the same larger team, and that if any part of the team fails, we all fail. We share a common purpose and a common mission. Therefore, logic would state that one of the most important partnerships you can develop is a partnership with your clients.

I make it clear to my clients that my success is predicated upon my ability to help them succeed. I try to understand what they are being asked to accomplish and what they are being held account-able to do. I try to focus my team's energies and efforts in helping to support these objectives. We have very senior leaders in my organization that we refer to as client relationship managers (CRMs) who actually serve as business-unit CIOs. Their sole purpose is to understand the business they serve and act as a single point of value and accountability for the IT function for that unit. These CRMs live with the clients, work with the clients, and in many cases are viewed as part of the clients' team as much or more than they are viewed as part of IT. They are strong advocates for their clients and act as arbiters to help negotiate what their clients need with what our team is capable of delivering. I have invested a great deal of my own personal time developing both professional as well as personal relationships with key clients throughout the organization. They know that they can count on me to support their efforts and work with them for the good of the entire organization. There is no more important role for a CIO to play than to develop these key relationships.

Partnering with Your Executive Management and Board of Directors

As a CIO (or for that matter, any "C" level executive), you are part of the senior leadership of your organization. It doesn't matter who you report to, it's more important how you are engaged and perceived by your counterparts in the "C" suite. You are also expected to be a business leader and be able to keep your board of directors apprised of what you are accomplishing, how you are investing (not spending) their money, and what value your functional area is bringing to help your company accomplish its mission. Therefore, another key partnership you need to create is with your executive leadership team, as well as with your board of directors. They need to see you as approachable, understandable, engaged, and supportive of their efforts. They must be able to count on you to act as a business leader and a member of the leadership team, not as a rogue practitioner who performs some black magic that they don't understand or see the value of. You must speak their language, be comfortable in their world, and help them to become more comfortable in yours. It is imperative that you not only market the value you bring to their efforts but that you help to make key members of your team more visible and appreciated for the talents they bring to the table.

Sourcing—Expanding Your Team to Include Outside Partners

The days of hiring all of the skills and resources you need to effectively run a complex organization are a thing of the past. More and more CIOs need to be able to leverage relationships with third parties who have the specific knowledge of very narrow functional specialties in order to run their operations. Many of these partners may live and work in foreign countries and in different cultures. These people often interface directly with your clients and are as much a part of your team (and a reflection of your efforts) as the people who wear your company's badge and work in the same building you do. When clients call my help desk, they don't know (or care) if the person on the other end of the phone is a member of our staff, or whether the person lives in New York or Russia. All they know is that they called my team for support and either had a positive or negative service experience.

I have seen too many executives treat the vendors they work with as slaves. They think they are the masters who pay for the service and the vendor's people are their indentured servants who will do their bidding. But these individuals are people just like your staff. They have goals and dreams and personalities, and they want to work somewhere they are appreciated, recognized, and rewarded for excellence. I treat all of the people who work as an extension of my team as if they worked for my company. At the end of the day, they *are* working for me and need to know that they can expect the same consideration and support that I would afford my staff.

The other mistake I see executives make is treating negotiations like a zero-sum game. There has to be a winner and a loser. The goal is to squeeze the last penny out of the vendor. However, in a partnership, the focus is win-win. What do I need from the vendors I work with? What are their objectives? What can I do that would be of value for them? Perhaps I can trade a few percentage points of revenue for some goodwill and testimonials. Perhaps I can act as a professional reference to other prospective clients. What do they hope to get from the relationship (besides revenue)? What can they expect from me? If I treat their people like an extension of my staff, will that lower the management costs of having them engaged on my account? Only when both parties feel good about the relationship and about what they are extracting from it can you expect to get the most from the people you are working with.

This is also true when it comes to shared accountability. Are you quick to point the crooked finger of blame at your vendor partners? Or do you take the time to understand what is really going on and roll up your collective sleeves to address the issues?

Through the Lens of the CIO—The Unique Challenge of Offshoring

We live in a global society and conduct business in a global marketplace. This has created both challenges as well as opportunities for business leaders. One scenario that is both a challenge and an opportunity is offshoring certain outsourced technology services. We have leveraged offshoring for a number of services, including application development and level-one support. While this approach has served us well, there are certainly lessons learned based on challenges we have had to overcome during these engagements. Let me share what I feel as some best practices that have served us well.

There are two levels to an offshore relationship. One is the heads-down technical work that has to be performed to support your enterprise. The other is a solid understanding of your business and your expectations. In a very real way, any outsource partnership is an extension of your team. My clients don't know and don't care if the people they are dealing with are badge-holding members of my staff or are employees of a company located in India. All they know is that these are *Larry's people*. Therefore, when selecting an offshore partner, you should perform the same level of due diligence you would when recruiting and hiring an employee.

You hear a lot about issues related to language and culture when dealing with people and organizations in other countries. These issues are real. One way we have gotten around some of these issues is to work with companies who have a local management presence onshore and technical talent offshore. This allows you to help address the language issue. It also helps your partner to be able to better understand your corporate culture, how you play the game, and your expectations. We also have a local relationship manager who "gets us" and acts as an intermediary with their offshore resources. The other thing we do is break down work to its basic components so that the offshore technical staff is focused on doing the coding while members of my team are focused on understanding the business logic and rules that go into developing the solution. We handle the client relationship, the business analysis, and the project management. We ask the offshore team to do what they do best—develop code to meet very focused technical requirements.

Offshoring can be an incredibly cost-effective way to get meaningful results. Just be sure to have the right players play the right positions.

Networking in the Industry

There is an old expression that no man is an island. We live and work in a very complex global community where no one person has all the answers or access to everything he or she needs to be successful over time. As the old song goes, "You've got to have friends. . . ." Taking the time and effort to develop relationships with various constituencies within your industry will pay tremendous personal and professional dividends.

For many of us, the term *networking* conjures up visions of BS artists in $3,000 suits walking around shaking hands and "working the crowd." This visual is repugnant to most of us, especially those of us who are more introverted by nature. But networking and building relationships isn't about glad handing and running for office. It is about making yourself open to know other people and support their efforts. Whether that means mentoring a more junior executive, or writing an article for a trade journal, or offering to present on a topic at a local industry conference, or simply setting up the folding chairs at a major event, the focus of effective networking is on giving, not taking.

Let me share a personal story that might shed some light on the magic of effective networking. I have been an active member of the CIO Executive Council since its inception. This is a wonderful organization that supports the growth and success of CIOs and the IT industry in general. They have been very supportive of my career and I, in turn, have done my best to support their efforts. One of the things I often do is make myself available to speak at conferences they sponsor. Last year, I was asked by them to serve as the keynote speaker at a major IT conference in New York City. At that event I met a gentleman who was running the conference, and we developed a relationship. About six months later, he contacted me and asked if I would consider providing an endorsement for a book he and his partner had written. I read the manuscript and found the book to be an excellent resource, so I gladly endorsed the book. He was most appreciative and asked how he could repay my kindness. I shared with him that I was considering writing a book myself but that I had no contacts within the world of publishing and didn't even know where to start. He was kind enough to introduce me to the gentleman who helped publish his book. The result of this story is that you are reading a book published by one of the premier publishing companies in the industry—because two people who met each other developed a relationship and supported each other's efforts.

What can you do to support the manufacturers in your industry? What vertical industry group can you join to learn more about what happens in other companies and offer to support your colleagues who work there? Maybe a fellow CIO is struggling with a project that you have experience with. How can you help her? What knowledge and experience can you share to help people avoid hitting the same potholes that you encountered along the road?

This is a small yet big world, and it always helps to have friends and associates who like you and want to help you. I am not saying you should be Machiavellian about this! I am, rather, suggesting that I am a big believer in karma—when you help people and put good stuff out in the world, it has a tendency to come back in ways you didn't expect or see coming. We all need a little help now and then. When you are the person with the helping hand out to support your colleagues and others, the world seems to magically work better for everyone involved.

Lessons Learned

- No one can succeed alone! You need to develop effective partnerships to drive change.
- Transformation requires an empowered workforce that puts the goals of the team ahead of their own personal agendas.

(continued)

(Continued)

- The days of command and control are over! The twenty-first century workforce demands your partnership and engagement as a member of their team.
- You need to create a partnership with your team. You shouldn't be their coach—you should be their quarterback!
- In order to drive effective change, your clients must feel that they are partners in the endeavor.
- No executive can succeed without the support and partnership of the executive team and the board of directors.
- The days of treating vendors like indentured servants are over! Your outsource relationships should be viewed as an extension of your team and you should aspire to create win-win relationships with all external partners.
- Networking with other people in the industry allows you to draw on an expanded set of resources and wisdom.

CHAPTER 9

Developing the Qualities of a Great Leader

A ll great leaders have certain qualities that provide them the ability and credibility to lead teams of people. In this chapter we will examine those qualities. Specifically, we will focus on the following concepts:

- ❐ Being authentic
- ❐ Inspiring others
- ❐ Building trust
- ❐ Showing humility
- ❐ Having a bias toward action
- ❐ Leveraging the collective wisdom of the team
- ❐ Building personal relationships
- ❐ Influencing others as a key characteristic
- ❐ Showing humanity
- ❐ Empowering people
- ❐ Being receptive to feedback
- ❐ Being likable
- ❐ Being accountable
- ❐ Having integrity

Although many great leaders may seem larger than life, it is important to remember that we are all just people and that, by definition, means we are all flawed creatures. There is no one, regardless of how successful or respected he or she may be, who is outstanding in every possible regard. Therefore, when reading and reflecting on the following list of qualities, it is important to understand that these are all important areas for us to work on, but that even the greatest leaders can improve in one or many of these areas. Our focus shouldn't be on becoming despondent because we aren't necessarily gifted in some of these areas, but, rather, to be cognizant of these qualities and make a concerted effort to improve on each of them on a daily basis. I once read a statement that said, "Success is the sum of small efforts repeated day in and day out." Please remember this when reviewing these leadership qualities and simply focus on improving your awareness and effectiveness in each of these areas.

Being Authentic

Early in my career I became fascinated with leadership. I developed a mental picture of what a great leader looked and sounded like. I envisioned a leader requiring the communication skills of Martin Luther King Jr., the motivational skills of Knute Rockne, the toughness of George Patton, and the human touch of Mother Teresa. Needless to say, with this as a benchmark I became quite concerned about my ability to ever aspire to a leadership position. Early on, I also tried to find great leaders I respected and tried to emulate them. I quickly learned that this approach was an unmitigated disaster! The truth is that I was not born with the looks and grace of President John Kennedy, the intellect of Albert Einstein, or the comedic genius of Robin Williams. However, I was fortunate enough to have a couple of decent qualities that I worked hard to fine-tune. What I quickly learned was that for me to be effective as a leader of people, I had to be . . . well . . . me! However I also learned that while I had to be myself, I had to be my best self!

Perhaps one of my earliest recollections of acting like a leader came when I was 15 years old. I had always loved music and had taken some basic lessons on how to play the guitar. I was born with a fairly good singing voice and, coupled with my new prowess (loosely speaking) on the guitar, I joined my first band—Psychotic Urge! I was in the band about four months and realized that we were going nowhere! The drummer was the leader of the band. His girlfriend was the lead singer. The only problem was, she couldn't sing! The lead guitarist was a friend of mine from high school who was talented but more focused on getting stoned than getting us gigs. No one was pulling together a set list or arrangements. No one was trying to market us and get us jobs. Practice would be a huge jam session where we would stumble onto a song or two and waste most of our time deciding what to play next! For a Type-A OCD person like me, this was surely hell on earth!

One night in a fit of disgust, I left band practice and went to hang out with my friends. None of these guys played an instrument, but all of them loved classic rock music (not that we called it that back in the 1970s!). In a moment of utter frustration, I loudly announced to my friends that we were going to start our *own* band! I told Vito he would learn to play bass; I told Sal he would play guitar; Mike would learn to play keyboards and Tommy would take drum lessons. In retrospect, this was at best delusional! None of these guys had any musical training, no less the money to even buy the required instruments and take the necessary lessons. However, for whatever reason—maybe due to the passion with which I delivered my message, maybe because of the trust I had developed with these guys, or maybe because they were just plain bored and looking for an adventure—they all took the bait! We did indeed create a band that played together for five years, and because of this experience we are all still dear friends 35 years later.

Looking back on this experience, I now realize why I was successful. I tapped into my own personal leadership style and played to my strengths. I was passionate, persuasive, supportive, and made these guys actually think we could succeed and look forward to the journey. The key is that I was authentic. I was being who I am and leveraging my own personal gifts. Each of us has different strengths and gifts. Great leaders are authentic because they are themselves. They don't try to be something they are not. They simply work hard to fine-tune their existing strengths and play to them.

Perhaps the best way to hammer this idea home is with another example. Over the past few years, both Tony Dungy and Bill Cowher have led their teams to Super Bowl championships. Both of these men are regarded as great coaches and will probably one day wind up in the Pro Football Hall of Fame. They both coached winning teams that were threats to win it all many times. However, that is where the similarities end! Tony Dungy is a very religious and dignified man. He is soft spoken, reflective, thoughtful, and very much the opposite of the loud, brash persona we often think of as a football coach. He is more of a father figure who is helping his players grow as men and learn from his teaching. Bill Cowher is quite a different personality. Nicknamed "The Jaw," he is as hard as nails. He's a passionate, loud, and fiery coach who is not afraid to get in his players' faces. His flow of words can be so impassioned and bombastic that he has been known to actually spit on players because he is so close to their faces and exuding so much energy! Neither style is more effective; each man's style has been effective because he has been authentic and true to himself. Could you imagine Tony Dungy suddenly screaming expletives at his players? Can you envision Bill Cowher holding hands with his players and saying a quiet prayer? Their players wouldn't know what to make of it! Effective leaders are authentic and play upon their personal assets to inspire and engage the people around them.

Inspiring Others

I just used that scary word again—*inspire*. This is a word that I had a hard time getting comfortable with. After all, we are IT executives. We are not religious leaders or heads of state. What we do can be viewed by the outside world as well . . . not necessarily inspiring? However, each of us in our own way needs to inspire the people we lead. We need to help them understand why what they do matters. We need them to see the linkage between their daily efforts and the big picture. They need to buy into the overarching mission of the organization and feel that they are doing more than making a paycheck—they are contributing to something that matters. We need to help them feel good about the contributions they are making to our organizations and to their loved ones. They need to have a sense of motivation that says, in essence, "I matter because what I do matters."

All leaders, regardless of their calling, need to feel a sense of purpose and share that purpose with their people so that they feel there is meaning in their work and dignity in their efforts. Otherwise, we are nothing more than indentured servants who are eking out a living and running on a treadmill! Do your people feel inspired? Do you even feel this is your responsibility? What can you do to make them feel a part of a larger purpose?

I routinely have guest speakers from our business present to my team at our staff meetings. They share their objectives and focus and also let the team know how what we do helps them accomplish these objectives. This not only makes the team feel like an important part of the overall organization but also helps them connect with the people we support. What have you done recently to inspire your people?

Building Trust

One of the most important qualities required for effective leadership is the presence of trust. I'm not talking about some exercise of falling back and having your colleagues catch you. I am taking about genuine "I've got your back" trust.

When I started in my current position, there was little trust with the people I inherited and their management. Management had decided to outsource the entire IT function and had kept the staff in the dark regarding this process or the rationale behind the decision. People were hanging around on deathwatch, waiting for the other shoe to drop. The first thing I was told by my new manager was that there was a severance budget and that I should simply fire all of the existing staff! I quickly explained to her that while it was possible that the people were a part of the existing problem, I needed some time and effort to work to understand what the real underlying issues were and to develop a plan to address them. I asked her to hold off for a couple of months before simply executing all of the employees!

Needless to say, the team I inherited was understandably not very trusting of management. They felt like they had been thrown under the bus and that no one was watching out for them. In conversations with my new team, I learned that many of them were bright and talented people. However, they were either not being used in the right roles or didn't have the support or processes in place required for them to be effective. Furthermore, my predecessor did not engage them in decision making and they were kept in the dark about where we were going, why we were going there, and how we planned to get there. I quickly shared with them that I had a different approach and that if they were willing to support my new approach, I had their backs and would make sure that they had what they needed to succeed.

This all sounds very kumbaya! However, what would happen when the rubber hit the road? They soon found out. Two events happened within the first couple of months that helped my team understand where I was really coming from. The first was a major systems outage. Many of our systems were old and antiquated and we had not invested wisely in keeping them state of the art. There was also little in the way of support processes to help keep systems working effectively. About a month into my tenure, a major system failed. The natives were restless! Everyone was gearing up for a fight. My people were waiting for me to throw them under the bus. They also expected me to start screaming at them.

The first thing I did was call my operations manager into my office. I asked him what had happened and why. I elicited his suggestions on how we could address the issue and what we could do to prevent a reoccurrence. When he finished speaking, I thanked him for his input and expressed my appreciation for his efforts to address the situation. He sat there for a minute waiting for the storm that never came. He finally got up and left my office, looking somewhat confused and very surprised. I sent out an e-mail message to our clients stating what had happened, what we were doing about it, and the steps we were taking to ensure it didn't happen again. I finished the message with the statement that I was accountable for all IT services, and that anyone who wanted to share concerns or displeasure with these types of issues should feel free to reach out directly to me. I shared that my people were working hard to improve things, and since I was accountable, I should be the focus of any energy regarding this or any future issue.

The second experience happened a couple of weeks later. We finally got an important project completed and the client group in question for the first time ever was very satisfied with our efforts! Everyone expected me to take a bow and share how the savior had made this happen. Instead, I publicly thanked both the members of my team who were engaged in this effort as well as our partners in the business with whom they had worked. People started to see that I had two very simple rules for the way I would lead and manage their team:

1. Give your people the credit for any success you experience.
2. Take responsibility for failure.

This is a recipe I highly suggest to any leader. It has served me extremely well over the course of my career.

Showing Humility

Mac Davis once sang a song that said, "Oh Lord it's hard to be humble, when you're perfect in every way."[1] While this is a comical lyric, the concept of humility is a serious item. All of us want to be appreciated and recognized for our efforts and our gifts. We all crave recognition of our successes. However, as I stated earlier, when you are a leader it is never about you. *Leadership is a responsibility, not a privilege.* Many people seem to forget this. They aspire to positions of leadership looking forward to the perks that come along with it. They want the glory. They want the attention. They want the nice office and the big salary. I have seen many a fine professional ruined by the development of what I refer to as *big head syndrome.* They actually start believing their press clippings. They become full of themselves. Instead of focusing on how they can serve and support others, they become focused on what's in it for them.

Great leaders have humility. Servant leaders focus on others and not on themselves. Humility is not an easy trait to have, especially when you have reached some level of success. It is a little easier for IT executives since IT can be a rather humbling way to make a living! We must always remember that with power and influence come great responsibility. Are we using our position and our influence to help others grow and meet their objectives? Are we focused on making our clients accomplish their goals or on who gets the credit when they do? When a team wins, there is plenty of credit to go

---

[1] Mac Davis, "It's Hard to Be Humble," *It's Hard to Be Humble* (Casablanca, 1980).

around. Focus on supporting those around you and this will come back to you in spades in the way of goodwill and appreciation from those you serve.

Servant leaders focus on how to make the lives of others easier, better and more productive. The most obvious aspect of this service mentality is the desire to support the business objectives of your clients, management, board, and other key stakeholders. Perhaps a less-obvious aspect of having a service mentality is to focus on the needs of your own team to ensure that they have the tools, support, guidance, and motivation they require to function at an optimal level. A true leaders' mentality is not that people work for them but that they work for their people.

Having a Bias Toward Action

Excellent leaders are men and women of action. They see an issue, identify the alternatives, and act to address it. One of the worst diseases rampant in corporations is the paralysis of analysis. People are aware of a problem but spend inordinate amounts of time analyzing all the angles and all the alternatives. They form a taskforce to look at the problem. Then they bring in outside consultants to provide feedback on how to address the problem. When all is said and done, a year has gone by and nothing has changed! Now don't get me wrong, I am not suggesting that a leader should shoot from the hip without an understanding of the issues or feedback from key voices on how to address them. I am simply stating that this process must be performed expeditiously and that once a leader has a feel for the situation, she must act.

My oldest daughter inherited some of my unfortunate traits (and fortunately, some of her mother's wonderful traits as well!). One of them is that she is a perfectionist. When writing a paper in high school, she would labor over it and work to produce the Michelangelo of all term papers! Unfortunately, this would become such a time-consuming effort that it blocked out potential time for all other endeavors (such as assignments in her other classes!). I shared with her that 80 percent of something is much better than 100 percent of nothing! There is a law we are all familiar with called *the law of diminishing returns.* This suggests that while you may be able to improve a decision or approach by an extra 10 to 20 percent, the time and resources required to accomplish this improvement are normally not worth the investment. Leaders should keep this in mind when making decisions.

The other mistake I have seen people make is to not make a decision. Sometimes people are indecisive because they genuinely don't know what to do and feel paralyzed in taking action. Other times, I've seen people simply hope the problem will go away! However, not making a decision is, in essence, a decision in and of itself. Indecision has consequences just like decisions do, and many times the consequences of indecision are even more dire.

My mother had a thyroid situation when I was a kid. She was petrified of doctors and secretly feared that she might have thyroid cancer. So she let it go and didn't deal with it. This resulted in her dying suddenly at the age of 53 years old from an utterly curable illness. Two years ago, I had a scare with my thyroid. Remembering the tragedy that befell my mother, I immediately went to the doctor. He sent me to a specialist, who biopsied some nodules on my thyroid. They came back benign and I was told to simply come back annually to keep track of things. The doctor told me that even had the biopsy been malignant, thyroid cancer is one of the most treatable cancers and if addressed quickly and effectively, it almost never leads to fatality.

This is a perfect analogy to how good and poor leaders deal with problems. Good leaders address them head on, quickly, and decisively. In most cases, they catch the situation in time to turn things around and the organization winds up with a "clean bill of health." Indecisive leaders hope the problem will go away, think about it too much, and often don't take action until it is too late. This can result in dire consequences.

The other reality is that it is easier to make a decision, find out it was wrong, regroup and make a new decision than it is to recuperate from indecisiveness. One of the things I admired about President Obama's early speeches is his honesty in saying that we need to try a number of things to turn the economy around. Some of them will work, some of them won't. We will learn from the ones that don't and make additional decisions. No one can fault a person who is trying hard and acting swiftly and decisively to address a situation. However, it is much easier to get upset if Nero fiddles while Rome burns!

Leveraging Collective Wisdom

I learned very early in my career as a leader that I didn't have all the answers. I also learned that being human, I had (sometimes gaping!) holes in my skills and experiences. That's why my priority has always been to recruit and retain talented people who have the skills and experiences that I don't. Andrew Carnegie had inscribed on his tombstone "Here lies a man who knew how to enlist the service of better men than himself." If this is true of Andrew Carnegie, how much more true is it of you and me!

I try to surround myself with bright, talented people—people smarter people than me (granted, in my case that's not so hard!)—and maximize their collective talents. Many leaders surround themselves with people just like themselves. Perhaps it's because this makes them comfortable. Maybe it's because they like people with the same qualities they possess. Whatever the reason, it is a mistake. I once worked with a very bright and talented executive who was a tremendous speaker and sales-man. He had a silver tongue and his focus and success were based on his talent in selling ideas and stories. Unfortunately, he surrounded himself with other talented salespeople but no one who could actually execute! The group had wonderful ideas and plans but nothing ever got delivered.

I draw from the people on my team to give me ideas on how we should do things. I know I am in trouble when everyone agrees with me! The higher a leader rises in an organization, the more he is surrounded by yes men and women. This is very dangerous. Someone needs to be able to tell the emperor that he has no clothes! You need opposing points of view, and your people need to feel comfortable that their opposing thoughts are not only tolerated but that they are welcomed!

Leaders take the careful time and effort to surround themselves with talented, experienced people and take their counsel very seriously. They are not too proud (or arrogant) to think that they have all the right answers or all the innovative ideas. They realize that the true power of any team is leveraging the collective brainpower that is assembled and that the human capital he has assembled is the most powerful asset and engine for success at his disposal. I tell my team, *"We are smarter than me."* What is the point to hiring intelligent, talented people if you don't intend to leverage the collective experience and acumen of the team? You are doing yourself and your organization a great disservice.

Part of this dynamic is also empowering people to make decisions and take actions. My people know that my role in the process is to help set a direction, articulate a vision, and provide them the resources and support they need to get things done. Then I need to get out of their way! They know if they need my support, I'm around. They know when they accomplish their objectives, I will ensure that they are recognized for the achievement. They also know that I am not going to micromanage them throughout the process. A leader sets the destination for where we need to go and allows her people the leeway to decide how to get there. This is hard for the control freaks among us (of which group I am a charter member), but it is absolutely critical that you give people the freedom to be creative and get the job done, even if you would do it differently.

Finally, a leader is honest about the fact that he does not have all the answers. There is a fine line between confidence and arrogance. A good leader is confident in her ability to engage her people and make good decisions based upon the input of the team. However she is not arrogant enough to think that she will always be right and that every serve will be an ace! The greatest champions are not those who never make mistakes, but those who can collect themselves and recover from mistakes.

Tiger Woods is an incredible golfer. He may very well be the greatest golfer of all time. Although he certainly possesses great talent, the real differentiator is his mental toughness. How many times have you seen a golfer who is having a great round hit a bad shot and wind up in a bunker? Normally, this sends the golfer into a mental tizzy and not only does he have a bad score on that hole but struggles the whole round. I have seen Tiger Woods hit the ball into trees, bunkers, who knows what. He collects himself and focuses on hitting a great next shot. He is a Houdini on the golf course, always getting himself out of trouble. Great champions and leaders make mistakes. They simply recover from them better than most.

Through the Lens of the CIO—Admitting and Learning from Your Mistakes

I am often amazed at how many leaders feel that they should never show any signs of being human. One of the real taboos for many leaders is admitting to their mistakes. They feel that to do so would be interpreted as a sign of weakness. I find this to be the pinnacle of hubris!

Last time I checked, we are all human beings. That means we are all flawed. It's important to realize that the only way to
(continued)

(*Continued*)

avoid making mistakes is to never attempt to accomplish any-thing! The more you take on, the more aggressive your agenda, and the more innovative your focus, the more likely you are to make mistakes. It is inevitable. Trying to run an innovative orga-nization while attempting to keep a perfect track record is a little like trying to hit home runs while never striking out. Not a very realistic scenario.

I make lots of mistakes. I am as flawed as anyone you will ever meet. But I view my mistakes as part of my education. I try to learn from them. I try to not repeat the same mistakes (a bit of a challenge, since I am thick headed!). I also apologize to my team (gasp!) when I've screwed up with them. My people know I am human. They know I screw up. However, they also know that I am approachable and that I will not throw them under the bus when they (inevitably) make their own mistakes.

Many mistakes are made out of ignorance. You are trying something new or a new way to address an issue. There is no road map or manual highlighting all the steps from point A to point B. Parents learn this the hard way, as our children don't come with an owner's manual! You learn to accept the fact that you will screw up and that, barring some huge mistake, your kids will probably survive just fine and won't need ten years of intense therapy.

As the old saying goes, the road to hell is paved with good intentions. The same principle applies at work. When you make a mistake, admit it. Apologize to the impacted parties. Share with them what your intentions were, what you learned from the experience, and how you hope to handle the issue differently moving forward. Clear the air and then move on. We often hold lessons-learned postmortems after major proj-ects. It helps us to learn from the experience, to capitalize on developing repeatable processes for what we did well, and reinvent approaches to what we executed poorly. It helps ensure that we don't keep making the same mistakes and getting blindsided by the same types of issues.

How many people never reach their greatest potential because they are quietly harboring ill feelings for some perceived wrong that was done to them? Their manager "threw them under the bus" or passed them over for a promotion or didn't recognize their contribution. They carry these indignities with them, and it stifles their contribution and the team's effectiveness. How hard is it to honestly deal with these feelings, to apologize when you made a mistake or handled something poorly, and put these types of emotions in the past? Do you think your people will think less of you if you fess up to being human and screwing up? Do you think they expect you to be perfect? As a leader, you often have to be the rock for your people. That doesn't mean you have to be a rockhead!

Building Personal Relationships

I have often heard people in formal leadership positions state that it is a mistake to get too close to your people and develop a personal relationship with them. I have a slightly different perspective. Now let me be clear. I am not advocating that your employees should be your drinking buddies! I'm not saying taking your people out for tequila shots is an appropriate team-building exercise! However, I do believe strongly that in order to get the best from people, it is important to understand who they are, how they are wired, and what makes them tick. This requires taking the time and effort to build a personal connection.

People are often amazed at the low level of attrition my teams have had over the years. In truth, virtually the only people who have ever separated from my organization are people who we decided to separate. It is a rare occurrence for team members to come into my office to tell me that they are leaving the team. I am very proud of that fact. The main reason why our retention rate has been so high is because we have taken the time to build personal relationships with the members of the team. Let me explain.

Many people feel that employees either take a new job or leave their old job because of compensation. Indeed, there are times when this is the case. In my entire career, I can count on one hand the times when I have lost good people because of money-related issues. Now keep in mind that for much of my career, I have led teams in either not-for-profit or mid-sized organizations. Therefore, it is rare than the members of my team make more working for me than they could in a larger company or a more technology-intensive industry. I can remember the time when a valued member of my team told me that he was just offered a job with a 40 percent pay raise. He had a daughter in college and a son on the way and felt he had to take the job. Even this person was reluctant to leave us. Why is that? Research has been done over the years that shows that compensation is rarely the most important variable in employee retention. More important in the minds of most employees is the relationship with the people they work for and with.

If you talk to ten people and ask them what matters to them most, you are likely to get ten different answers. All of us have unique needs and motivators. What is important to me may be of little consequence to you. Knowing what people value is an incredibly powerful piece of knowledge in ensuring that you can create a value proposition that resonates with them. Building a personal relationship with your people allows you to know what matters to them so that you can effectively motivate and support their needs. It's important to know that Pete's daughter is in ballet and that he enjoys going to her recitals. Giving him the flexibility of schedule to attend these events is probably more important to Pete than a $10,000 raise would be. Being aware that Anne has a two-hour commute to work (not atypical for many people who work in New York) and allowing her to work in her home office three days a week is probably a compelling perk for her. Knowing that John's child has special medical needs and ensuring that your health plan can provide the benefits required to care for him means a great deal.

The only way you learn about what motivates people is by taking the time and effort to build a personal relationship where they let you inside of their world and help you understand what matters to them. When you know what matters to people, you can better ensure that their needs are being met. When people's needs are met, there is a greater sense of loyalty and appreciation and you will get more from them than someone who is simply punching a clock to pay the bills.

One of the perks of working in my field is that I get to be up close and personal with some of the greatest tennis players in the world. A leader can learn a lot from watching these world-class athletes. One year during the U.S. Open we had a team meeting the week before the event in our player dining area. This is a lovely facility with a great view overlooking our practice courts. When we arrived at the meeting around 10:00, I noticed Andre Agassi working out on the practice courts. Andre was by far the oldest player in the men's draw that year. He was already a multiple Grand Slam champion with a Hall of Fame career. Andre had nothing to prove. I enjoyed watching him hit with his partner but soon refocused my attention on the meeting at hand. The meeting lasted about 90 minutes. When we finished the meeting we all went to grab some lunch and went back to our table. We enjoyed lunch, had a nice conversation, and were ready to leave the area and get on with the rest of our day. Before I got up to leave, I turned to take a peek to watch the action on the practice courts. There was Andre, still out there working as hard as he had been two hours ago.

Great basketball players such as Michael Jordan are famous for being gym rats. They are the first ones in the gym and the last ones to leave. Arguably, no one in the history of the NBA had as complete a set of skills as Michael Jordan. ESPN rated him the greatest athlete in history. He was also the hardest worker in the NBA. Even with the incredible skills he possessed, he dedicated himself to perfecting his craft. If someone as gifted as Michael Jordan felt the need to exhibit this level of dedication, what does that suggest to the rest of us mere mortals? I've used this quote before and I will use it again, "Success is the result of small efforts repeated day in and day out."

I once watched an interview with Muhammad Ali. Ali was aptly called the greatest of all time. He possessed a combination of speed, grace, intelligence, and power that were unique in the world of boxing. During the interview, Ali stated that every fight he ever won or lost was won or lost before he ever stepped into the ring. The victory was in the preparation and the arduous roadwork that was performed at early morning hours in nondescript gyms, not at Madison Square garden in front of a worldwide audience.

Greatness requires dedication. It requires continuous improvement. It requires focus and effort.

Influencing Others

Very few people have enough power to ram their agenda through. Even the president of the United States, arguably the most powerful person in the world, has to motivate both houses of Congress to support his legislative initiatives. If you look at every organization, there are people who hold titles and people who actually hold the power. While there is a certain level of power that comes with a title, respect does not necessarily come with the title. People have deference for the office, but they have respect for individuals. The people who really get things done in any organization are able to lead due to their influence.

There are many reasons leaders may have influence in an organization. Perhaps they are viewed as a subject matter expert in an area that is valued by the people around them. Perhaps they have a proven track record of execution that makes their words carry more weight. Maybe they carry themselves in such a way, generating such goodwill, that a request from them will certainly garner support. Whatever the reason, it is imperative for leaders to understand the power of influence and learn to develop the characteristics that create this influence.

Showing Your Humanity

Somewhere along the line it became fashionable for leaders to be seen as aloof and impenetrable. The idea was that effective leaders were tough, single-minded individuals who were impervious to the same emotions that impact mere mortals. Now I totally understand the need to be unflappable under pressure. I also see the value in being the rock that people gravitate toward when the storm hits. However, somehow in our quest to be seen as strong, many leaders have lost the ability to be human.

People respond to people—plain and simple. If you look at the relationships in our lives, most of us try to surround ourselves with people who make us feel comfortable and allow us to be ourselves. We don't much enjoy the company of robots who don't exhibit any passion, energy, or emotion. Being "emotional" is often perceived as a very negative thing for a leader. We must be strong. But if you want to get the most out of people, you must be seen as human. You must be willing to let down your defenses and let other people know who you are as a person.

I'm not suggesting that you should be going out with your staff to karaoke Fridays at the local watering hole. I am suggesting, however, that you allow people to know who you are and what makes you tick. If something is wrong, instead of trying to gloss over it, deal with it. Let people know that you recognize the issue and what you plan to do about it. If you make a mistake, admit it! I always marvel at so-called leaders who refuse to apologize to their "subordinates" (a term I absolutely hate!). They view it as being weak. Well, let me let you in on a little secret . . . we all make mistakes! The only way to avoid them is to do nothing, which is often the biggest mistake! When you do make a mistake you should be enough of a person to admit it. Let me share with you a statement I want you to memorize and use as often as necessary (especially if you are married!):

"I screwed up. I'm sorry. How can I do better next time?"

There is an old saying: *"People don't care how much you know until they know how much you care."* Being human and letting people see who you are, with all of your warts and blemishes, makes you real. It makes you approachable. It makes people feel like they can talk to you. Many leaders try to separate themselves from their teams. They feel that they are the general manager and the rest of the team are the players. I have a different approach. I am a member of the team like everyone else. It just so happens that I am the quarterback of the team. That doesn't make me any more or less important. It just means I play a more visible position where too much credit is given when things go well and too much blame when things go poorly. My team knows that I am one of them. I face the same challenges and have the same problems that they do. I'm one of them in every way that matters. They also know they can come to me with problems because they won't be judged or yelled at. They will be listened to and supported.

Empowering the People around You

I don't believe in babysitting unless the people in the room are under the age of 12. Too many leaders feel that they know best and that their answers are the right answers. I have almost 30 years of experience so hopefully I've learned a few things along the way. That doesn't mean I'm always right. It doesn't mean I have all the answers and it certainly doesn't mean that people need to do things my way every time.

I have a very simple management philosophy. It has served me very well and perhaps it may be of value to you as well. Recruit and hire talented people with great attitudes. Work with them to understand what your vision of success looks like and what needs to get accomplished. Provide them the tools, resources, and support they need to accomplish the objectives. Then—and this is the most important part—get the heck out of their way.

I have seen many leaders who take great pride in the fact that they have to bring their laptops with them on vacation because the team could never survive without them. They wear this as a badge of honor to show how important they are. I view this as an incredible sign of poor management. You hear a lot about the CIO having to develop business relationships and work with key constituents. How do you suppose a CIO is able to do that if she is spending all of her time worrying about keeping things running?

I have a very talented team. They know their jobs better than I do (by the way, if the CIO is the most technically adept person on the team you probably have a problem on your hands). They know where they can find me if they need me. They know that when they are attacked, I have their backs. They don't need me to micromanage their efforts. If you have a situation where people are being micromanaged, you either hired the wrong people or hired the wrong manager. Empower people to make decisions. As a matter of fact, most effective organizations push decisions as far down the food chain as they can. If you see an organization where decisions are bottlenecked at the top, you know you have an inferior management culture. My people know that they can do what needs to get done without having to ask, "Mother, may I?" Do yours?

Being Receptive to Feedback

Good leaders are receptive to feedback. Their people aren't afraid to tell them bad news for fear of retribution. One of the biggest challenges a leader has when moving up the organization chart is that he becomes farther separated from the real world of customers and issues. Leaders must keep a finger on the pulse of what is happening at a grassroots level. Although part of the solution is to remain engaged with customers, another part is having the members of your team who are living in this reality day in and day out be willing to share with you how your program is playing in Peoria.

People know that I literally and figuratively have an open door. As an aside, I once worked for a woman who said she had an *open-door policy.* However, her door was always closed, and even when it was open she had situated her office with the back of her chair to the door so she didn't have to see you coming. People know that it's more important to tell me what I need to hear than what I want to hear. A leader knows he is in trouble when he finds himself surrounded by yes men and women telling him how brilliant he is. If people think I'm brilliant, I've obviously chosen the wrong people! As a leader, you must be in touch with the real world. There is no better way to do this than by having a reputation as someone who welcomes the truth.

Being Likable

You may be asking yourself what this topic is doing in a leadership book. What's so important about being likable? And is there any place for this trait in business?

Do you watch *American Idol?* It's OK; no one can see you raise your hand—it's just you, me, and this book! My wife loves *American Idol* and I love my wife. Therefore I love *American*

Idol. I grew up playing in rock bands, and to this day I play in a band that performs classic rock music. I am the lead singer in my band. While I am not giving up the day job anytime soon, I do know a little bit about what good singers should sound like. Now I have noticed in the last couple of seasons of watching *American Idol* that while the best singers often go far in the competition, they rarely win. Two years ago, the final came down to Adam Lambert and Kris Allen. Both of these were talented and good-looking young men. For those of you unfamiliar with these two performers, Kris is more of a balladeer with a very pleasant voice and a boy-next-door demeanor. Adam is far more flamboyant and in-your-face. He has a voice that could be described as being the second coming of Freddie Mercury (lead singer of Queen before his death). His vocal range is ridiculous; on a few occasions, my garage door opened during his performance. Both gentlemen did their best during the finals of the contest, but it was pretty clear to the judges (as well as to me) that Adam was the superior vocalist. However when the votes were tallied, Kris was named as that year's *American Idol.* I asked my wife who she had voted for, figuring she was a good litmus test of the American voting public. She told me, to my surprise, that she had voted for Kris. When I asked her why, she said, "Adam has a better voice, but I like Kris."

I worked for a major Fortune 100 firm for almost ten years. At a certain level, people became stock eligible so promotions to this level were viewed as important enough to enlist the opinions of the candidate's peers. I sat in on a number of these conversations. I rarely heard any conversation about the person's technical acumen or project management capabilities. I did hear an awful lot about "I like Joan; she's a nice woman." "I enjoy working with Bob and his team." Even in these important discussions that determined promotions and equity decisions, the likability factor was far more important than almost any other characteristic that was discussed.

Being Accountable

It goes without saying that leaders take accountability for both their actions and outcomes. They don't look for scapegoats to pass the buck. They don't expect someone else to step up and do the dirty work. Leaders roll up their sleeves and do what needs to be done. They have the conviction to take a stand when they think something needs to be done. When there is a problem, leaders own it. They ultimately feel that they have a personal stake in the company and are responsible for ensuring its success and progress. The mantra of a real leader is, *"If it is to be, it's up to me!"*

You can learn a lot about people if you watch how they handle success. You can learn even more about them by watching how they handle failure (or at least temporary setbacks). A real leader makes sure that when things go well, the team receives all the credit, recognition, and reward for success. Leaders ensure that they are advocates to market the great work and progress their teams make. They ensure that their partners in the business units who sponsored the projects receive the credit and recognition they deserve for their contributions. Leaders focus on everyone except themselves. Their reward is seeing their people and their partners bask in the light of their well-deserved victory.

The time a leader needs to be the center of attention is when things go poorly. I often tell my team that my job is to make sure they get credit when things go well and to fall on the grenade when things go poorly to ensure they don't get hot with the shrapnel. Leaders don't point fingers. They don't throw anyone (especially their people and their partners) under the bus. Leaders absorb the negative energy and shield their people so that their team can focus on the challenge at hand. Leaders run political interference and act as the human piñata. Leaders are fully accountable—period.

The Most Important Characteristic of a Leader—Having Integrity

There is an old expression that says, "What you do speaks so loud I can't hear what you say!" Integrity is really about walking the talk. How many people do you see espouse a certain approach from their perch only to personally take a different road? How many televangelists and politicians preach the moral high ground, only to be caught in the web of lies and deceit? Integrity is the most important underpinning of any true leader.

My people know that I'm not the smartest, most talented, or handsome guy in the world (by a country mile!). But they do know that if I say something, you can take it to the bank. People who know me know what makes me tick. If you invite me to your house for dinner at 7 P.M., you can expect your doorbell to ring at 6:45. If you don't hear from me by 7 P.M., call the police to put out an all-points bulletin and call the hospitals. My word is my bond. I screw up with the best of them. I make lots of mistakes (anyone who actually tries to do something often will) and I have more flaws than the average bear. But you can count on me to do what I tell you I'm going to do. Integrity says that what I feel, what I say, and what I do are congruent and consistent. That's really all you can truly ask of anyone.

Lessons Learned

- Great leaders are very different in many ways. They have unique personalities and styles. However, they share some common characteristics and values, which include:
  - Authenticity
  - The ability to inspire the best in others
  - The ability to build trust in people
  - Humility and a servant attitude

(continued)

(*Continued*)

- A strong bias toward action
- The willingness to listen to others and leverage the collective wisdom of the team
- The ability to build relationships and influence others
- Showing your humanity
- An ability to empower others
- A positive receptivity to feedback
- Likability
- Accountability
- An overriding sense of integrity that comes through in everything they say and do
- These are not traits you learn once and forget! They must constantly be honed and practiced.
- Even the greatest leaders stumble sometimes. The key is to go back to these principles and work to make them second nature.

CHAPTER 10

Sustainability

Leaders come and go; organizations—if led correctly—endure for generations. In this chapter we will discuss how to sustain good leadership. Specifically, we will focus on the following concepts:

☐ Getting to the top of the mountain is only the beginning!
☐ Individual leadership only gets you so far.
☐ There is a need for a culture of leadership.
☐ As a leader, job one is creating other leaders.

In every field of endeavor from business to sports, there are surprise teams who pop up every now and then to win a championship, only to fall back to the pack the following year. Then there are teams who consistently exhibit the qualities that it takes to compete at the highest level on a consistent basis. Getting to the pinnacle takes a lot of time and energy. Staying there, however, is the true test of exceptional leadership. It is not very common for a Super Bowl winning team to repeat this accomplishment. However that is the goal of great leadership.

Accomplishing Short-term Success Is Only the First Step

Many of us inherited truly dysfunctional organizations that required years of discipline and sweat to turn around. Many of the experiences and suggestions found in this book are focused on that initial journey from being a "cellar dweller" to improving to become a .500 team, to ultimately arriving at the pinnacle of being a truly world-class organization. Many leaders at this point take a deep breath, rest on their laurels, and enjoy the fruits of their labors. Although it is certainly appropriate to appreciate your progress and bask in the glow of success, this should be a brief moment of celebration before getting back to work!

Inertia is a powerful force. Breaking the grips of inertia and getting an object in motion takes a great deal of energy. Making sure the object is propelling in the right direction takes focus and wisdom. Once you have a head of steam, it is far easier to keep progress on track. However, many people spend too much time on *emotional vacations* where they forget the effort and drive it took to get to where they've arrived. The danger is that if you stop for too long, you have to go back to step one and break through the wall of inertia all over again.

My wife tells me that I am like a shark; if I ever stop moving, I will die. There is a lot of truth to this statement. While I occasionally slow down to "smell the roses," I am careful to never stop. My job is never done, since perfection is an impossible goal to achieve. We are always trying to get a little bit better. There is always a new challenge to embrace and another mountain to climb. IT can be a very humbling area of endeavor since stuff can and will go wrong. This helps keep us humble.

Another issue some leaders face is that they start to believe their press clippings. You get a little recognition, maybe receive an award or two, get published in a trade journal, present at a major industry conference. People want to know what you think. Others want to know how you accomplished your objectives. After a while, you start to think, "Hey, I'm the *man!*" This is an absolute trap. In my introduction to this book, I shared with you that I consider myself a lifelong student of leadership, not an expert. There are people who've forgotten more about leadership than I've ever learned! I am not delusional enough or arrogant enough to think I have all the answers. I've had a lot of experience and made a lot of mistakes. I've seen what seems to work and not work, and can share my personal perspective and suggestions with you. This doesn't make me smarter, better, more talented, or more successful than you or anyone else. It just means I've lived through some battles and am happy to share the tales. Thinking that you've made it is a guaranteed kiss of death. Hopefully, you aren't willing to settle for the progress or success you've earned to date. My hope is that my best days are still ahead of me and that I still have something to accomplish, lots to learn, and plenty of people to support. This is my perspective on progress. I hope you share it.

Individual Leaders Can Drive Short-term Success

I have seen organizations who are led by incredibly talented and charismatic leaders accomplish a certain level of success and fame. These people are often very exciting to be around. You often see them on the media circuit—Heck, some even may show up on *Oprah!* Others are like the Pied Piper. They are leading the parade and everyone else is following them around. People become infatuated with them. In essence, every industry or field of endeavor has its own rock stars.

This is all great. There's only one problem. Eventually, this "messiah" retires, or dies, or gets a big head and moves on to what he or she believes to be greener pastures. If the organization has not been thoughtful and careful, this can leave a leadership void that creates a sucking sound that is deafening. Some people start companies from scratch, work their whole lives to build something of value, and then turn it over to their children. Within two generations, many of these companies go from nothing to success and back to nothing. The next generation doesn't have the same focus, work ethic, or drive that the founder had in creating and running the business.

I grew up in a blue-collar neighborhood in Brooklyn, New York. A man in my neighborhood started a contracting business and built enough success to move his family to a much nicer area and provide his children the education, opportunities, and best things in life, which he had never had access to. When his oldest son got married, the man gave the son the business as his wedding present. About a month later, I saw the newly married son driving around in a brand-new, candy-apple-red Corvette convertible. Nice car, I thought—but who's watching the shop? Sadly, this business is no longer in existence. Unfortunately, I can't say that I'm surprised.

You Need a Culture of Leadership to Ensure Long-term Viability

Long-term success is very difficult to sustain. It certainly cannot be accomplished based on the talents and acumen of a single individual, regardless of how good she is. Real sustainable success requires the development of a culture of leadership.

It is my responsibility to develop a leadership culture. There is a line in a song by Augie Nieto that says, "It's not the breaths you take, its how you breathe." Clearly, getting results is always important in business. But the process as to how you get the results is often more important than the results themselves. I have worked in many places where "the ends justified the means." I have seen leaders "take the hill" only to wipe out all the villagers in the process. It is imperative that you set an example for your people and model for them how to play the game. They should be able to watch you and learn how to handle the challenges they will encounter on the road to success.

176

In the 1990s, many Christian teenagers wore T-shirts and bracelets sporting the acronym WWJD. This stood for "What would Jesus do?" Now I am not advocating any particular religious belief. I am not suggesting that leaders are as important as or can aspire to be as perfect as Jesus, and I am not trying to be sacrilegious. However, I do think that there's a point to be learned from this approach. Your people watch you. Hopefully, you model the behaviors you want them to emulate. When they are faced with their own challenges and are left alone with their thoughts, hopefully they ask themselves the questions, "What would Joan do in this situation?" "What would Carlos do?" The idea is not for them to make the same decisions you would or to have the same strengths and weaknesses that you have. Rather, the focus is on the process of how you have helped teach them to play the game.

A Leader's Job Is Not Only Creating Success—It is Creating Other Leaders

Finally, as a leader your most important job is to develop other leaders. I have people in my organization who I am certain will be CIOs someday. At every level in my organization there are leaders in development. It is a priority for me to ensure that these talented people have the opportunities, visibility, access, and support they need to develop their skills and ascend to greater levels of contribution. I never worry about the "ship" when I am away from the office because I know that my team is at the wheel and they are incredibly competent and capable of keeping things progressing in the right direction. I know that when I decide to leave the organization, there is no chance of it going aground because we have developed leaders at every level of the organization who know how to get results and the right way to get them. I have total confidence that they will continue to thrive and drive value long after I'm fishing from a charter boat somewhere on the Gulf Coast.

Through the Lens of the CIO—Leaving a Legacy

As you get older, you start to think about how you have spent your life and what you have accomplished. You start thinking about what your legacy will be once you are gone (sorry if I just freaked you out or sent you into a spiral of depression!). No one lives forever, and no leader stays in a position forever. You do your best and then move on. What is the legacy you hope to leave as a leader?

Most of us will never have the impact of Mother Teresa or Dr. Martin Luther King Jr. We will never change the world or invent the cure for cancer. Perhaps the greatest legacy I personally saw a single person leave was the legacy left by my mother. She was a very simple woman with a high school education who never worked in a big organization or held a position of power. Yet when she passed, the funeral home had to close the rest of the chapels to handle the overflow of people who came to pay their respects. A number of people on the staff of the funeral home were overheard asking, "Who was this woman?" The plain truth of the matter is that my mother left everyone she met better off for having known her. She was kind, selfless, and always had a positive and encouraging word. She went out of her way to help people with no expectation or desire for her kindness to be returned. She made everyone feel better, made their day a little brighter and their load a little lighter. In a small way, she left the planet better than she found it.

What do you want your professional legacy to be when you retire? I can tell you very simply what my answer is to that question. First of all, I want my organization to continue to be successful and feel the positive impact of the progress we made well after no one in the company even remembers my name. I want to ensure that the culture we built and the changes we implemented can be sustained and built on. I want the company to be more successful ten years from now than it is today. Second, I want to see the people who worked for me become some of the best leaders in the industry.

A while back, I started providing executive coaching services to sitting and aspiring CIOs. I can assure you that I am not getting rich from this effort and that my motivation was not to put a down payment on the yacht! The payoff for me is seeing a light bulb go off when one of my mentees sees a way to deal with a challenging issue. My reward will be seeing members of my team become successful CIOs who make a difference for their companies and the overall industry. I hope to see some of the people I coach show up on the cover of major trade magazines. Finally, I hope that many of the people who I have led and who I have mentored "pay it forward" and help to develop and support the next generation of CIOs and IT leaders.

What do you want your legacy to be? What are you doing about it?

Lessons Learned

- Individual leadership can help accomplish short-term success, but it only goes so far.
- In order to sustain long-term success, you must develop a pervasive culture of leadership.
- The most important thing a leader can do is to develop other leaders.
- Your leadership legacy will be measured by what happens after you are long gone!

CHAPTER 11

Homework and Parting Thoughts

So you've made it this far—congratulations! Hopefully, some of what you have read to this point has resonated with you and you have had a *light-bulb moment* or two along the way. When I work with my executive coaching clients, I always leave them with a few parting thoughts, as well as with some homework assignments to help ingrain the concepts we are working on. Over the years, I have also become somewhat "infamous" in my organization for espousing what people have come to refer to as *Larry-isms!* I leave you with a few of these thoughts (some which we've discussed before) that will, I hope, stay with you and help guide you on your leadership path.

Leadership Begins with Me!

I have often heard people complain about the fact that they would be better leaders but for the fact that they work for an idiot! Always remember that leadership begins with me. No matter what is happening above me or to the side of me, I can and should set the example for how the game should be played. No excuses . . . no whining!

I *am* IT!

When I took my first CIO position, I had a number of truly significant cultural challenges to address. The most important was to instill a culture of accountability. My motto and the motto I suggest every member of your team take on is simple . . . "I am IT!" Anything that happens in IT matters to me. Any problem that we are having is my problem. If I can't help resolve it myself, I will reach out to someone who can. If a client has shared a concern with me, he or she has spoken to IT, and therefore, I will help connect the person with someone who can make a difference for them. I have 100 percent ownership for the success of my team because I *am* IT.

Be Wary of Linda Ronstadt Disease

Some of you might be old enough to remember Linda Ronstadt. Linda was a very popular and talented singer who had a number of hits in the 1970s (yes, I am that old!). One of her hits was a song called "Poor, Poor, Pitiful Me." I have worked in organizations where people have developed whining to an art form. All of us have challenges. All of us struggle at times. However, moaning and groaning (while it may feel good at the time) rarely adds any value to helping solve our problems. As a matter of fact, it can emotionally immobilize us and preclude us from taking the actions required to address the issue. Be wary of this disease, and make sure that you don't get infected with it yourself.

Seek Alignment versus Consensus

I have worked for organizations where a lot of people have input into decisions and a decision may not be final until consensus is reached. *Consensus* is at best an elusive goal, even for a small group of people. Asking a large number of people to agree in anything (even where to go for lunch) can be a frustrating exercise. Therefore I am a firm believer in *alignment*. On most issues, I will gather my leadership team and elicit their input. More often than not, I will go with the prevailing decision that the team suggests. However, there are times when my experience, my political awareness, or my gut tells me that we need to take a different tack. I always provide people the opportunity to share their ideas, suggestions, approaches, and concerns. However, once we arrive at a decision (whether or not it would be the way I would do it), we expect all participants to fully support the decision and rally all of their energy, acumen, and support to make it work. This is called *alignment,* and it is one of the cornerstones of any high-performing team I have ever seen.

God Gave You Two Ears and One Mouth

My mother, God rest her soul, used to tell me (often), "Larry, God gave you two ears and one mouth—use them in that proportion." When we become leaders, we sometimes become drunk with the elixir of power and begin thinking that people are actually listening to us! That makes us believe we have something important to say.

Many times, people struggle trying to understand how to figure out what other people want or expect of us. My experience has been that people will tell you everything you need to know about how to effectively work with them if you will only shut up and listen to them. Ask any of your business analysts how they determine requirements for new solutions. Then ask them what percentage of their time they spend talking versus listening.

How Do You Feel When You Are the Customer?

A few years ago, I was watching my favorite hockey team, The New Jersey Devils, play in game six of the Stanley Cup finals. Two of the Devils were coming in on a two-on-one breakout when suddenly my cable went out! Needless to say, I was not amused. I called the cable company and, after being placed on hold for 20 minutes (Why do their messages always say your call is important to them when clearly if it was, they would answer it faster?), a "representative" asked about my problem. It was very clear after a few moments that this person was highly unmotivated and could not care less about my issue. To me, at that moment my problem felt like the most important thing in the world (which, clearly, it wasn't).

Conversely, I had a very different experience flying on Virgin Atlantic Airlines. After a brutal week on business in the United Kingdom, all I wanted to do was plop in my seat and watch some movies. The personal video system on my seat was working but I had no audio. The flight attendant replaced my headphones, crawled under my seat to try to tweak some wires, but to no avail. I resigned myself to the fact that I wouldn't be able to watch a movie. He came back in about a minute with a Sony Watchman and a list of movies available on that format, stating that he was sorry for the inconvenience but hoped that I would be able to find movies on this format that I would enjoy! See the difference?

Always remember how you feel when you are the customer and make sure you treat your clients in a way that you want to be treated. Something about a golden rule. . . .

Leadership Is a Responsibility, Not a Privilege

Too many people feel that having a position of leadership and authority is their God-given right. They feel superior to those in their employ or at so-called lower levels in the organization. All too often, I have seen a certain level of arrogance and entitlement exhibited by people in leadership positions.

Ask anyone who has ever played the quarterback position in football who the five most important people in the world are to him, and he will tell you it is the offensive line. These are athletes who don't get anywhere near as much of the publicity, credit, or salary that the quarterback does. However, watch a left guard miss a block and you will see just how successful the quarterback is while laying on his back with a 300-pound linebacker on top of him!

Leadership is not a privilege. It is a responsibility. Leaders are accountable for the success and livelihoods of dozens, hundreds, or thousands of people. They should always remember this fact and never act in a cavalier fashion. The decisions they make, the actions they take, and how they carry themselves impact a large and diverse community. They should be humble in their demeanor and focused on serving their constituents, not being the big shot on campus.

You Are Either Part of the Solution or Part of the Problem—the Choice Is Yours

I firmly believe that in life, you are either part of the solution or part of the problem. I have seen many people who started out as positive contributors become jaded or cynical and start gossiping or talking badly about management. Everything is wrong and everyone is stupid. No one knows what they are doing. The place is a joke. Sound familiar?

For these people I have the following suggestion—either put up or shut up. There are certainly times when things in an organization are being run in a suboptimal fashion. If you have a suggestion that can possibly improve the effectiveness of the team, then step up and make it. If there is a talent or experience that you possess that can benefit the team, then offer to share it. Otherwise, shut up! As my mother often told me, "If you have nothing good to say, then say nothing at all." Every day, ask yourself the question, "Am I part of the solution or am I part of the problem?"

There Are Three Kinds of People in the World

I am also a believer that there are three kinds of people you will encounter in life:

1. *People who make things happen.* These are the doers, the movers and shakers. They are at the center of progress. When you see a lot of activity and progress, these people are never far from the action. These are the people who truly are responsible for making the world run and for running the world.

2. *People who watch things happen.* These are the spectators in life, the armchair quarterbacks. They have "all the answers" but are never part of the solution. They always have the answers though they've never applied them, and can tell you how to do something better though they've never attempted it. In the words of Theodore Roosevelt, "Far better is it to dare mighty things, to win glorious triumphs, even though checkered by failure, than to take rank with those poor spirits who neither enjoy much nor suffer much, because they live in a gray twilight that knows not victory nor defeat."[1]

3. *People who wonder what happened.* They are the poor, oblivious souls who are not engaged enough to be part of the game so they live their lives in the dark and allow other people to set the agenda and make decisions for them.

---

[1] Theodore Roosevelt, "The Strenuous Life," speech given at the Chicago's Hamilton Club, April 10, 1899. Accessed at www.historytools.org/sources/strenuous-abridged.html.

Through the Lens of the CIO—Congratulations! You've completed the course! Now it's time to start all over

So you've come to the end of the book—good for you! Hopefully, you read all the way though and didn't skip to the end.;-)

I believe strongly that learning is a lifelong process. Everything that is alive is either growing or dying. Only you can decide which category you fit in based on the decisions you make and the actions you take. I hope you have come away from the experience of reading this book a little wiser, a bit more prepared to lead your organization, and perhaps a bit more inspired to take on the challenges that come with the territory. I can assure you that in writing this book, I have to constantly relearn many of the lessons I have shared with you. We are all a work in progress, and that progress is never a straight line. In the immortal words of Bruce Springsteen, we all take one step up, two steps back.[2]

I hope that you keep this book by your desk and refer back to it time and again. I hope you loan it to a colleague. I hope you remember to give yourself and the people you work with the benefit of the doubt and have the wisdom to know that we are all flawed creatures who have to continue to learn life's lessons and figure out how to incorporate what we learn into how we live and act. Every person's journey is unique. I hope that yours is filled with joy, discovery, challenge, and success.

When You Change, Your World Changes

This is the final thought I will leave with you for your consideration. I spent a lot of time over the course of my life and my career being unhappy about how other people were acting or living

---

[2] Bruce Springsteen, "One Step Up," *Tunnel of Love* (Columbia, 1987).

their lives. I spent a great deal of energy trying to change other people and get them to see the folly of their ways (and, of course, the brilliance of mine!). Whenever life was not going the way I wanted it to, I would blame other people for it and moan that if only they would change, things could be so much better.

I'm embarrassed to say that it took me well into my fourth decade of life to realize that, first of all, I had neither the right nor the ability to change anyone else. All people have the right to be who they are, see things the way they see them, and act the way they deem appropriate. No matter how stupid, wrong, or destructive they seem to me in my infinite wisdom, I have no right and very little ability to impact the way they think or act.

However, there is one person who I can change. That person is me. This is not an easy task, either, as I am set in my ways, have my own set of biases, and my own lenses through which I see the world. Anyone who thinks it's easy to change themselves should reflect back on how difficult a time they've had in changing their diet, breaking a bad habit, or modifying the way they interact with their significant other. No, changing yourself is certainly not easy. But at the end of the day, you are the only person you have any chance of changing.

However, something magical happens when you do change yourself. Everything around you also seems to change. When you decide to be more patient, the people who used to drive you crazy no longer seem to have that effect. When you decide to work on your personal areas for development, your wife or husband seems to be more reasonable and easier to get along with. When you try to develop empathy and learn to see things from the other person's perspective, suddenly they become less adversarial and more human. It's amazing—just try it! When you change, it seems the world changes around you.

We are all human and, by definition, flawed. Everything you have read in this book you will need to learn and relearn many times. You will become adept at certain qualities but struggle with others. You will never perfect any of these qualities. I am as flawed as the next guy—probably more so! Just because I wrote this book certainly doesn't mean I don't need to read it and apply the lessons myself. I mess up with the best of them! Leadership development is a lifelong process. Embrace it. Become a student of it. Work at it like your success depends on it—because it does!

About the Author

Larry Bonfante has held executive leadership positions over the past 29 years in the financial, pharmaceutical, not-for-profit, consulting, and sports and entertainment industries. Larry holds a master of science degree in organizational leadership and has received numerous industry accolades, including being named as one of *Computerworld*'s Premier 100 IT Leaders in 2009. As Chief Information Officer at the United States Tennis Association, Larry's team is responsible for all information technology related services supporting the U.S. Open, the most highly attended annual sporting event in the world. Larry has served as a mentor and executive coach for many IT leaders in various industries. He is the founder of CIO Bench Coach, an executive coaching practice that focuses on helping IT executives realize their potential by transforming the human side of IT leadership.

Larry has served as a mentor and executive coach as part of the Pathways program for the CIO Executive Council. He has also served as both president and chairman of the Fairfield-Westchester chapter of The Society for Information Management. He has been a guest lecturer at Columbia University, New York University, and Polytechnic Institute. He is an accomplished public speaker who has presented at many industry conferences and writes a monthly leadership column and blog for CIO Insight magazine.

You can contact Larry at Larry@CIOBenchCoach.com. To learn more about his executive coaching practice visit his website at www.CIOBenchCoach.com.

Index